DYNAMICS OF HUMAN HELPLESSNESS

Advances in Psychological Research in India Series

1. Perspectives on Psychological and Social Development—*U.N. Das* and *Udai Jain*
2. Psychology of Poverty and Disadvantages—*Girishwar Misra* and *Ajit K. Mohanty*
3. Perspectives on Indigenous Psychology—*Girishwar Misra* and *Ajit K. Mohanty*
4. Psychology of Reading—*Shantilata Sahu*
5. Personality Issues by Assessment the Projective Approach—*P.K. Rath*
6. Dynamics of Human Helplessness—*Fakir M. Sahoo*

About the Author

Dr. Fakir M. Sahoo is Professor in the Centre of Advanced Study in Psychology, the first of the two such Centres in India. He received Canadian Commonwealth Scholarship and received doctoral degree from Queen's University at Kingston, Canada. He worked with Professor John W. Berry the past-President of International Association of Cross-Cultural Psychology. His other achievements include University Grants Commission's Career Award in Humanities and Social Science, Indo-Shastri Fellowship offered by Shastri Indo-Canadian Institute, and Professional Associateship accorded by East-West Centre, Honolulu, Hawaii, U.S.A. He has published several books. His publications include titles such as *Affective Sensitivity and Cognitive Styles, Psychology in Indian Context, Environment and Behaviour, Cognitive Styles and Interpersonal Behaviour, and Child Rearing and Educating Assistance Manual* (CREAM). He has published approximately 60 research papers in national and international journals. In addition to supervising a large number of M.A. and M.Phil. dissertations, he has completed supervising more than twentyfive doctoral theses. He has directed five national seminars/workshops. Apart from presenting a large number of papers in regional and national conferences, he has presented papers in more than 20 international congresses. These include his chairmanship in a session of the International Congress of Psychology held in Brussels, Belgium. He has visited countries such as Canada, U.S.A., U.K., France, Japan, Germany, Belgium, Holland, Spain, Switzerland, and Turkey. His voluminous writings (both in academic and popular press) in regional language have brought him several literary awards.

Advances in Psychological Research in India Series—6

DYNAMICS OF HUMAN HELPLESSNESS

FAKIR M. SAHOO, *Ph.D. (Queen's)*
Professor of Psychology
Centre of Advanced Study in Psychology,
Utkal University, Bhubaneswar, India

CONCEPT PUBLISHING COMPANY, NEW DELHI-110059

ISBN 81-7022-948.0

First Published 2002

Published and Printed by
Ashok Kumar Mittal
Concept Publishing Company
A/15-16, Commercial Block, Mohan Garden
NEW DELHI-110059 (India)

Phones: 5351460, 5351794
Fax: 091-11-5357103
Email: publishing@conceptpub.com

To

Professor Chittaranjan Das

whose writings have inspired many to combat helplessness.

PREFACE

The monograph *Dynamics of Human Helplessness* is a product of a programmatic research spanning over two decades. The major support for this research came from the University Grants Commission (UGC) of India in the form of a *Career Award in Humanities and Social Sciences*. The opportunity helped to give undivided attention for a continuous period of three years (1987-1990). This assistance was also useful in devising assessment materials and conceptual tools. Subsequently I was privileged with a research grant from the Indian Council of Social Sciences and Research (ICSSR). This was instrumental in my pursuit of looking into the correlates of helplessness. Finally a grant from the National Council of Educational Research and Training (NCERT) helped me to carry out studies on remediation programmes. I am grateful to these agencies for their support. However, the views and opinions expressed are mine and do not reflect the views of these agencies. I am grateful to Professor Emiritus R.N. Kanungo, Faculty of Management, McGill University, Canada for his helpful suggestion.

My doctoral students offered me the benefit of academic networking. Their efforts and thoughts provided bits and pieces in the structural growth of my work. I wish to thank Dr. Jayalaxmi Das, Niranjan Sia, Bidyutprava Tripathy, Chittaranjan Mohapatra, Mihir Kumar Sahoo, Abantika Kar, Sanchita Nanda, Padmini Paikray, Trupti Nayak, Binita Nanda, and Major Satya Narayan Ray. I thank Pradeep Mahapatra, Banchhanidhi Mallik, Pabitra Majhi, and Akhay Kumar Das for assisting me in various forms. I am also thankful to Professor A.K. Mohanty, the Former Coordinator, and Professor A.S. Dash, the present Coordinator, Centre of Advanced Study in Psychology for their support.

Finally, I would like to indicate that working on a project of this nature is not without unpleasant encounter with helplessness and hopelessness. Yet, the constant support system provided by my wife, Reeta, and my daughter, Voomika, was a force within to overcome the hurdles and to keep up the spirit of struggle. I owe a lot to them.

F.M. SAHOO

CONTENTS

LIST OF TABLES

1

INTRODUCTION

Involvement with the process of life is central to human existence. Humans are not just breathing, eating and breeding animals; they participate in the process of on-going changes. Social evolution is facilitated by diversity of human activity.

However, the spurt of activity drops down when people are afflicted by helplessness. Helplessness imprisons people in the cell of passivity. These people display gloom and demonstrate inactivity. Helplessness syndrome not only creates a condition of immobility for the individual, it brings in its train various forms of collective impoverishment.

A major form of such impoverishment concerns the problem relating to the growth of competence in children. Studies of growth have employed a number of developmental perspectives. Most of these perspectives have been addressed to the role of positive correlates of development such as McClelland's (1961) notion of achievement motivation. The studies of growth have also emphasized socialization pattern that fosters children's competence. The studies of achievement motivation have shown that mothers' independence training fosters achievement strivings in children (Winterbottom, 1958). Similarly, Witkin's studies of psychological differentiation have shown that masterly training given by mothers fosters autonomous strivings in children (Witkin & Berry, 1975).

Although these perspectives have identified the role of certain competence-inducing factors, an examination of negative forces such as the experience of uncontrollability is likely to offer new insights into the problem. The literature on mental health indicates that the management of positive affects and negative affects produces quite distinct, although related, effects (Bryant & Veroff, 1984). Similarly, it is plausible that helplessness plays a distinct role in the impairment of children's competence (Sahoo & Sia, 1988).

More specifically, socio-cultural systems of developing countries present conditions that are indicative of severe resource constraints. In such situations, people are likely to experience more uncontrollability compared to people in the developed countries of America and Europe. It appears that the construct of helplessness would provide indigenous explanation of people's adaptive styles in the developing world. This is also the case with Indian socio-cultural system.

The psychology of passivity can best be comprehended within the framework of learned helplessness. The phrase "learned helplessness" first was employed by Overmier and Seligman (1967) and Seligman and Maier (1967) to describe the debilitated escape-avoidance response of dogs exposed to uncontrollable shocks in the laboratory.

In the typical animal experiment, rats learn to jump to the safe side of the platform when such animals are placed in the unsafe side which is electrically charged. During 1960's, M.E.P. Seligman and his colleagues in the University of Pennsylvania got curious to investigate the effects of noncontingent conditions. Both the sides of the platform were charged rendering the entire setting as inescapable. The exposure of animals to this uncontrollable situation led the animal find out escape route initially but later found that there was no escape. Following a prolonged exposure, the animal exhibited learned helplessness in the sense that organism did not learn to escape to the safe compartment even if it was made safe.

Thus, learned helplessness is a reaction to conditions of uncontrollability resulting from the perception and/or learning that responses and outcomes are independent. Once developed, helplessness deficits are manifest in three interrelated areas of functioning: cognitive, affective, and motivational. The cognitive deficits are manifest in terms of associational deficiencies; organisms fail to learn association between new stimulus and response. The acquisition of skills is made impossible. Second, organisms display depressed affect. A depressive posture sets in following the experience of uncontrollability. Third, there is retarded initiation of responses. The organisms learn that all attempts to solve a problem is an exercise in futility.

While the initial studies were confined to specific animals such as rats and dogs, subsequent investigations documented helplessness syndrome across a wide variety of animals. In the context of man, a fourth deficit came to the fore. It was shown that humans experience self-esteem loss following their exposure to uncontrollability.

The typical learned helplessness experiment involves a triadic design. In this arrangement, the first group of subjects is exposed to uncontrollable events. A second group yoked to the first group is exposed to controllable events of same intensity or a duration, while the third group is not exposed to such event. Subsequently, all these three groups are tested on a controllable events. The comparison of "give-up" responses during this test phase demonstrates helplessness phenomenon; the phenomenon predicts that the first group would not be able to control the event whereas other two groups would be able to control.

Hiroto's (1974) study is a typical illustration of human helplessness experiment. A group of college students were exposed to loud controllable noises which they could terminate by pressing a button four times. Another group of college students were exposed to uncontrollable noise that terminated independently of their responses. A third group of subjects were not exposed to this event. Later all these three groups were tested on a hand-shuttle box where noise control was possible. Subjects were asked to terminate noise. The results confirmed the predictions of learned helplessness model. Subjects exposed to controllable noise or no noise could terminate the noise whereas subjects exposed to uncontrollable noise failed.

However, exposure to uncontrollable events is not sufficient to produce helplessness deficits. While experiencing uncontrollability, the organism must come to expect that responses and outcomes are independent. Thus, the expectancy that responses and outcomes are unrelated is a very critical factor in the induction of helplessness deficits.

The other important feature of helplessness syndrome is its cross-situational consistency. Helplessness induced in one specific domain may get generalized to other task domains. For instance, helplessness is induced by exposing subjects to uncontrollable loud noise condition. Following the experience of uncontrollability in such instrumental domain, subjects may be tested on a cognitive task such as mathematical problem solving. The impaired performance in this cognitive domain is indicative of helplessness deficit. Similarly, helplessness induced by exposing subjects to unsolvable mathematical problem may lead to the debilitated performance on controllable loud noise.

The Gaps in Early Conceptualization

While the original learned helplessness theory provided a framework of understanding cognitive, affective and motivational deficits as a result of the expectation of response-outcome independence, its critical examination revealed a number of inadequacies.

Helplessness and Locus of Control

The first issue involves the relationship between learned helplessness and locus of control. Rotter (1966) observed that people differed with respect to their belief regarding the source of reinforcement. According to Rotter, people with external locus of control believe that the causes of changes are external to themselves. Such causes are product of luck and chance. On the contrary, people with internal locus of control believe that they themselves are the causes of changes. Rotter's conceptualization of internality and externality provides initial impression that learned helpless individuals do have external locus of control whereas less helpless people have internal locus of control.

The verification of this presumed relationship between helplessness and external locus of control was attempted through chance-skill studies. If a task is skill-based, it is likely that individuals will show marked degree of change of expectation following success or failure. If a task is chance-based, subjects would show minimal change of expectation following success or failure. However, helpless as well as people with external locus of control were believed to treat skill-based tasks as chance-based. Accordingly they were predicted to show small change of expectation. The initial empirical studies confirmed these predictions, helpless individuals like persons with external locus of control showed small changes of expectation following success or failure. Yet, further analysis on the basis of post-experimental questionnaire revealed that both helpless and non-helpless subjects considered tasks of skills as matters of skills and success was considered predictable. So, the relationship between helplessness and locus of control is much more complex than supposed simple assumption that helplessness is positively related to external locus of control. The issue demanded research attention.

Similarly, Bandura (1977a) proposed that there are two reasons for people's "give-up" responses. When people give-up, they may believe that they do not possess capabilities; this denotes low self-efficacy. People may also give up because of their belief that the environment is unresponsive even though they have capabilities. This is indicative of low outcome efficacy. The relationship between helplessness and Bandura's conceptualization also needed clarification.

The Issue of Generality and Chronicity

The second issue concerned the problem of generality and chronicity. The original theory did not offer any explanation as to why different people exposed to specific uncontrollable situation would generalize their helplessness to new situations. For instance, people may experience uncontrollable (negative) events in their interpersonal lives; they may experience helplessness because they are betrayed by their friends. Following this experience of helplessness, some people limit their helplessness deficits to the original (personal in this case) domain whereas other individuals generalize their helplessness to work life. The original model of helplessness did not account for this individual differences.

Similarly, another question is also pertinent. Why do some people exhibit chronic helplessness whereas other people demonstrate helplessness deficits for a temporary period? The exposure to uncontrollable (bad) situations generates cognitive, motivational and affective deficits for some hours, days, may be for weeks. Yet, the intensity of these deficits gradually goes down for some people and eventually the deficits disappear. Yet, these deficits stay over months and years in the lives of some people. This great sweep in stability was an unsolved issue.

These inadequacies were subsequently handled with the revision of the helplessness theory. The current version is basically a reformulated model.

The Current Version

The current version of the construct of helplessness is stated in attributional terms. In fact, the February 1978 issue of the *Journal of Abnormal Psychology*, (Volume 87, Number 1) was specifically devoted to proposing, discussing and analysing the role of attributional dimensions in helplessness.

Types of Helplessness

The first inadequacy of the early version was solved by proposing a distinction between *personal helplessness* and *universal helplessness*. The expectation of non-contingency may pertain to the dimension of self; orthogonally it may pertain to the dimension of others. At one extreme position of contingency, there is non-contingency; at the other extreme, there is full contingency.

It is presumed that persons experiencing personal helplessness attribute causality to internal factors whereas individuals demonstrating universal helplessness attribute causality to external factors. Accordingly people demonstrating universal helplessness exhibit external locus of control; they believe that events are brought about by uncontrollable factors such as chance, luck and fate. On the contrary, persons experiencing personal helplessness believe that they do not have the controlling response, though others can control events. In other words, external locus of control is positively related to universal helplessness and locus of control as a construct is orthogonal to helplessness.

Similarly, Bandura's (1977a) low self-efficacy is akin to personal helplessness whereas low outcome efficacy is indicative of universal helplessness.

Attributional Analysis

In the revision of earlier version of learned helplessness, Abramson Seligman and Teasdale (1978) not only used the attributional dimensions of internality-externality to distinguish two types of helplessness, they employed two other attributional dimensions for solving the problem of inadequacy. These two dimensions include *stability* and *globality* Weiner (1974) has had previously introduced the attributional dimensions of internality-externality, globality-specificity, and stability-instability in the context of social behaviour in general and achievement motivation in particular.

Seligman and his associates employed these three attributional style constructs to revise the theory of helplessness. It was posited that individuals encountering uncontrollable situations ask themselves three fundamental questions. These three questions involve: (a) who is responsible for the bad event?; (b) how pervasive is its effect?; and (c) how long would it stay?

Every person is presumed to have a characteristic way of responding to these questions. The style of response determines the helplessness pattern.

It is possible that individuals may attribute the causality to internal factors. They may explain the negative events in terms of their lack of ability. On the contrary, they may explain the events in terms of the role of other individuals or outside factors (external attribution). Similarly, they may feel that the event would pervade into all aspects of their life (global attribution) or they may feel that the effects would be limited to specific domains of their life (specific attribution). Furthermore, some people may believe that the negative events would continue forever (stable attribution), while others believe that the events would be short-lived (unstable attribution). Thus, attributional styles, also called explanatory styles, may assume magnitudes along three dimensions.

Since these attribution styles are assumed to be independent dimensions, several possibilities exist with respect to their combination. For instance, a person may use internal global and stable attribution style whereas another person may employ external global and stable explanatory style.

In reformulated version of the theory of learned helplessness, internal global and stable factors for explaining bad events are considered insidious; they constitute the risk factors for the induction of helplessness deficits (Peterson & Seligman, 1984). It is observed that the revision brings to the fore a number of implications.

First, the attribution of internality predicts the type of helplessness to be induced. With internal attribution, the person is likely to experience personal helplessness. On the contrary, external attributions denote the unresponsiveness of external environment; the person experiences universal or shared helplessness. The distinction between internal and external attribution also explains the degree of self-esteem loss experienced by helpless individuals. Why should individuals blame themselves for failures if causal agents are outsiders? Accordingly, people with internal explanatory style experience guilt and self-blame and they show depressed affect. The degree of self-esteem loss is proportional to the internality of attribution.

The attribution of globality explains the pervasiveness of helplessness syndrome. With global attributions for explaining negative events, persons transfer their helplessness to new situations. For instance, a person may encounter a negative event in the form of an accident of losing a hand. With global attributions, the person believes that his or her life is doomed, nothing can be done. For such a person, helplessness spills over to many domains of his/her life. In similar situation, another person may use specific attribution and prevents generalization. It may generate the belief that the person can do many useful things by using several of his/her limbs, although the use of hand is not possible. Similarly, persons may limit the effect of negative events to a specific domain (i.e., work domain) whereas individuals with global explanatory style generalize from work to family domain. This generality of helplessness deficits is postulated to be proportional to globality of attribution.

Finally, the attribution of stability explicates the chronicity of helplessness. When people use stable explanatory styles for explaining bad events, they consider uncontrollable happenings permanent. Consequently helplessness deficits persist over time. On the contrary, people with unstable attributions regard bad events as passing clouds. For them, deficits are short-lived. The degree of chronicity is correlated with the magnitude of stability of attribution.

Seligman and his associates offer three categories of evidence to validate attributional model of helplessness. These include helplessness deficits induced and observed in laboratory conditions, attributional evidence, and chance-skill studies.

As argued earlier, helplessness deficits are postulated to exhibit cross-situational consistency. The reformulated version seems to answer why helplessness generalizes to new situations and survives the time gap between tasks. It is posited that globality and stability of attribution mediates the process of generality.

An illustrative evidence of this postulate is a study by Roth and Kubal (1975). Subjects were led to believe that they were participating in two separate experiments. However, participants of Group-1 were further told that their performance in Experiment-1 was predictive of their future college grades, whereas participants of Group-2 were informed that their performance in Experiment-1 was indicative of just their learning. Thus, a sense of importance was conveyed to Group-1 while a sense of relative unimportance was communicated to Group-2.

The performance on cognitive problem faced by all subjects in Experiment-2 was compared across groups. As predicted, Group-1 subjects showed greater helplessness than did Group-2 participants. The investigator's communication in the beginning was such that Group-1 subjects were likely to have global attributions and Group-2 participants had specific attribution. The difference in attributional style was thought to bring about a gap in performance in Experiment-2.

Similarly, Douglas and Anisman (1975) showed that failure on supposedly simple tasks produced greater helplessness deficits. It is assumed that failure on simple task is likely to induce internal attributions. When people fail on simple tasks, they tend to perceive that they do not have the ability (internal attribution). On the contrary, failure on complex task is generally perceived to be a product of interplay of external factors such as task difficulty. With this rationale, the investigators found that initial failures on simple task produced greater helplessness deficits compared to cases where initial problems were designed complex and subsequent ones simple.

The reformulation better explains the immunization effect in helplessness process. It is experimentally observed that initial success experiences make the attributions less global and therefore deficits less pervasive.

It is also observed that debriefing in experiments on helplessness reduces the intensity of deficits. Koller and Kaplan (1978) debriefed subjects participating in helplessness experiments. It was found that there was subsequent attenuation of helplessness deficits. When subjects are debriefed they learn that their helplessness is manipulated by experimental design. Accordingly their attribution of internality and globality is likely to change to externality and specificity. This change in attribution is likely to be reflected in the reduction of helplessness deficits. This has been empirically supported.

The second category of support includes attributional evidence. The theory of helplessness predicts performance deficits in both the conditions of personal helplessness (internal attribution) and universal helplessness (external attributions). However, expectation of uncontrollability would persist over time and situations when attributions are stable and global.

Tennen and Eller (1977) attempted to manipulate attributions to study their effects. They presented some unsolvable discrimination problem. In the first condition, the tasks were labelled progressively "harder." They reasoned that failure on easy problem would generate a sense of lack of ability (internal stable and global attribution). On the other hand, failure on difficult problems would generate a sense of task difficulty (external, stable and specific attribution). Subsequent to this manipulation, the investigators assessed performance of both groups of subjects in Experiment-2 as in the case of Roth and Kubal (1975) study. The predictions were supported. Subjects exposed to the first condition indicated greater performance deficits than did subjects exposed to the second condition.

In a different study, Hanusa and Schulz (1977) manipulated attributional styles. Subjects participated in a training task. Half of the subjects were led to believe that they were personally helpless (internal attribution) whereas the other subjects believed that they were universally helpless (external attribution). Subjects were subsequently tested on a test task. While the investigators did not find performance difference across groups, analysis carried out by Wortman, Panciera, Shusterman and Hibscher (1976) showed that subjects with personal helplessness indicated greater discomfort than did subjects with universal helplessness. Although the main findings did not support the prediction of the reformulated version, proponents of the theory argued that the tasks used in testing situations were not sensitive enough to show group difference.

In the context of attributional evidence Dweck (1975) examined attributional styles of the fourth grade school children who differed in terms of explaining their failure. Some attributed to the lack of ability whereas others attributed to lack of effort. The lack of ability was viewed as a factor of stability, the lack of effort was regarded as a factor of instability. Dweck and Reppucci (1973) found that girls attributed to the lack of ability and boys attributed to the lack of effort. Subsequent tests also indicated that girls showed greater deficits on test situations compared with boys. This was in congruence with the reformulated version of helplessness.

Third category of investigations cited in the context of attributional analysis of helplessness involves chance-skill studies. Generally it is found that normal individuals increase their expectancy of subsequent success following initial success; similarly they decrease their expectancy of future success following initial failure experiences. However, a number of studies (Klein & Seligman, 1976; Miller & Seligman, 1973) document that helpless and depressed individuals increase their expectancy for success less following success and decrease their expectancy of future success less following failure. Although these observations are cited as evidence of the reformulated model, there are complicating factors.

Weiner (1974) has argued that attributional dimension of stability is the determinant of expectancy change. According to him, attributions of unstable factors produce small expectancy change; attributions to stable factors produce large expectancy change. Accordingly, past performance would produce future outcomes to the extent past performance is believed to be caused by a stable factor.

Viewed from this angle, the direct measure of attributional styles of helpless and depressed subjects participating in chance-skill studies is likely to provide necessary proof. However, attributions of helpless subjects have not been directly measured in chance-skill task situations. A smaller range of expectancy change of helpless individuals relative to non-helpless persons can be interpreted otherwise. It is possible that the 50 per cent success pattern typically used in chance-skill studies may lead helpless subjects to believe that they lack the stable factor of ability but ability is not necessary for success on the task. After all, they succeeded sometimes in spite of their perceived lack of ability. Here, the subjects will show smaller expectancy changes, because they believe outcomes are a matter of chance (instable factor) for themselves, although they believe that the task is a matter of skill for others.

On the basis of this argument, Abramson, Garber and Seligman (1980) opine that small expectancy changes do not necessarily imply a belief in response-outcome independence and large expectancy changes do not necessarily imply response-outcome dependence. According to them, expectancy changes on chance and skill tasks do not directly test the learned helplessness model of depression. Nevertheless, the finding that depressives often show smaller expectancy changes on skill tasks than do non-depressives provide indirect and limited support for the model of learned helplessness. Thus, the direct test of attributions and greater range of chance skill studies are needed to generate definitive answers.

Despite gaps, a bourgeoning of research interest has been demonstrated in the area of learned helplessness. The breadth of interest has encompassed the ontogenesis and application domains of helplessness. Furthermore, the empirical research has raised the possibility of controlling human helplessness. Attempts are now directed to the explication of these issues and concerns.

2

DEVELOPMENT OF HELPLESSNESS

Developmental analysis of human helplessness presents a contrast to the oft-discussed concept of growth of competence. A large number of researchers have investigated the development of competence in general and growth of children's competence in particular. This has provided impetus for the advancement of several competence-related constructs such as achievement strivings (McClelland, 1961), competence motive (White, 1959), self-efficacy (Bandura, 1977b), control perception (Skinner, Chapman & Baltes, 1988), and action control (Kuhl, 1981).

While these approaches to the study of competence have generated much information regarding competence-fostering conditions, there seems to be a research gap with respect to the inhibiting forces. It appears that these positive factors of development work well in situations where conditions are optimal. These concepts lose applicability, atleast in part, when the socio-cultural system has much constraints. For instance, Sinha (1970) has shown that one-to-one relationship between a person's need achievement and accomplishment, as conceptualized by McClelland (1961), does not hold in India. This is because of severe resource constraints. Indian farmers have to depend on right kind of monsoon to have a good harvest. They have to rely on the genuineness of the store that sells seeds. Sinha (1970) argues that the perfect relationship between an individual's need achievement and success is bound to be moderated by the consideration of such resource parameters (Sinha, 1970).

On the contrary, complex and difficult environment requires some conceptual tools that are better suited to the analysis of passivity—the obverse of competence. The developmental analysis of helplessness offers immense possibilities for explaining such passivity in difficult and disadvantageous environment. Of course, it is posited that an understanding of such inhibiting forces is necessary to combat helplessness and promote competence.

Learned helplessness is an 'induced' personality trait. The prefix 'learned' emphasizes the point that a helpless individual has personal history and this history is necessarily a matrix of experiencing non-contingency (response-outcome independence).

However, studies of helplessness in the past were not geared to investigate its development. Studies of development require longitudinal investigation with a view to delineating the role of age-related factors. A heavy thrust on the manipulation of situational variables in experimental setting did not provide such a scope. Yet, indirect evidence was available with respect to the development of perception of control. Since perception following uncontrollability underlies helplessness, developmental studies of perception of control are considered important in this context.

There are several distinct lines of investigations that highlight the developmental aspects. Two broad classes of influences deserve discussion: familial origins and experiential antecedents.

FAMILIAL ORIGINS

Recent advances in technological innovation have made it possible to study the prenatal environment of the child. Although there are some studies to show that the new-born shows some specific preference for sound, odour and tastes as a result of its prenatal learning, the role of intra-uterine factors in helplessness has yet to unfold. However, post-natal experiences of the new-born have been examined. A number of factors seem to operate during infancy and childhood socialization period. A basic form of experience that seems to shape the infant's sense of helplessness is its early contingency situation.

Early Contingency

The role of early contingency in the development of perception following control has long been recognised. Seligman (1975) points out the possible effect of early contingency.

> I am convinced that certain arrangements of environmental contingencies will produce a child who believes he is helpless—that he cannot succeed—that other contingency will produce a child who believes his responses matter—that he can control his little world. If the child has been helpless repeatedly, and has expressed little mastery, he will believe himself to be helpless in a new situation, with only minimal cues. How easily, how many, and how

intense the experiences of helplessness and mastery are will determine the strength of this motivational traits (p. 137).

A number of early researchers have adopted Watson's (1966, 1971) paradigm of studying non-contingent situation. The paradigm makes use of a device. The device consists of a mobile suspended over a crib and attached to a pressure-sensitive pillow that can be placed beneath the baby's head or legs. The experimenter can determine whether the turning of the mobile would be activated by pressure on the pillow or whether it would turn independently on a prearranged schedule.

Watson and Ramey (1972) used this paradigm to investigate whether infants were able to perceive the contingency between their actions and environmental changes. They compared the effects of contingent stimulation (child controls mobiles), non-contingent stimulation (mobile turns independently) and no stimulation (mobile is stationary) on rates of responding. The responses of the 8-week old infants with contingent stimulation rose significantly over 14 days, relative to their own base rates. The non-contingent and non-stimulation groups did not increase rates of responding, nor did they differ from each other in the number of pillow activations.

Subsequently, Watson and Ramey investigated the generality of the phenomenon. They looked at the effects of non-contingency exposures on contingency learning using a variety of responses in training and test situations (e.g., panel pressing, arm pulling, vocalizations, discrimination learning). Studies of Watson and his associates led Franklestein and Ramey (1977) to conclude that "the present results support the conclusion of prior research that responsiveness is an important dimension following environmental stimulation influencing cognitive and social development in the first two years of life" (p. 817).

Lewis and Goldberg (1969) adopt similar views about the role of contingency in parent-child interaction. They see contingency as "the basis for all future learning" (p. 82). They view the caregiver's role as critical to the development of the child. According to them, mother is important because it is the contingency between the infant's behaviour and her responses that enable the infant to learn that his or her behaviour does have the consequence. In a study, Lewis and Goldberg examined the effects of maternal stimulation and response contingency in twenty 12-week old infants. The latency and consistency of maternal responses (look, touch, vocalize, smile, hold) to child behaviour (stare, move, cry, vocalize) were related to the child's cognitive development as measured by the speed of response decrement to repeated stimulation. Shorter latencies and greater responsiveness to infant cries and vocalization were related to more advanced cognitive development. They concluded that the generalized expectancy that behaviour is able to effect the environment is dependent on maternal reinforcement and short latencies.

Ramey, Starr, Pallas, Whitten and Reed (1975) used contingency as a basis for an intervention programme meant for severely retarded children. When compared to children who received only a nutritional programme, children whose mothers were instructed to provide experiences that made them aware of contingency between their own actions and external stimulations showed greater improvement in the Bayley Psychomotor Scale and in learning to use vocalizations to control stimulation.

Riksen-Walraven (1978) conducted a responsiveness intervention programme for the caregivers of 100 infants aged 9 months. Parental responsive behaviour and infant contingency perception were measured before and after a 3-month programme. Participants in the programme showed significant increases in responsive behaviour at the post-test. Participants also had infants who significantly more often learned the contingency Riksen-Walraven explained these results by assuming that the increased responsiveness following the participation in the programme raised their infant's sense of efficacy to successfully execute these behaviours which (a) lead to a generalized expectancy of efficacy and control, (b) increase infants' motivation and persistence in laboratory learning tasks, and (c) result in better performance on the task.

Apart from these studies, contingency has emerged as a core construct in parent-child interaction (Crandall, 1973; Lamb, 1979; Lefcourt, 1976). These authors view that contingency experiences of the infant not only shapes the infant's perception of control in the physical world but also in the social domain. The infant learns that its activity can produce desired changes in behaviour of others.

However, Skinner (1986) takes a critical view of this interpretation. She agrees that a "contingent" mother is one who responds quickly, consistently, and only to the target actions. Yet, she argues that contingency refers to response parameters, not content. To illustrate, she offers the example of a mother who slaps her child every time (and only when) it cries. This mother is as contingent as one who soothes it. From a control perspective, repeated exposure to these two cases are likely to produce in the child perception of contingency. However, their effects on child's affect, attachment and behaviour are obviously different.

Skinner (1986) views that an additional dimension is needed to account for these consequences as well as formation of generalized experiences of control. She termed this dimension *sensitivity* or *responsiveness*. It refers to the appropriateness of maternal event relative to the child's activity. Thus, the mothers described earlier can be differentiated not by reference to contingency but in appropriateness of behaviour.

Lamb and Easterbrooks (1981) have summarized studies of contingent sensitivity and they observe that:

> The contingent responsiveness of people has another major consequences for infants. From repeated occurrence of sequences in which the infant's behaviour serves as the stimulus eliciting a predictable adult response; the baby learns that its behaviour can elicit environmental consequences.... What occurs next is the most important development—the infant recognizes that it is effective, that it can elicit responses and thus partially determines its own experiences (p. 2).

Ainsworth and associates have further offered conceptual and operational definition of parental sensitivity. It includes both contingency and appropriateness. It "implies that signals are perceived and correctly interpreted and that response is prompt and appropriate" (Ainsworth, 1967, p. 198).

Several sets of evidence have been offered to support the hypothesis that cognitive and social development are intimately interrelated and that the maternal sensitive responsiveness influences both. A mother's prompt responsiveness to her baby's signals tends to foster the development of varied and clear modes of communication; thus the development of one facet of social competence is ensured. One such study by Bell and Ainsworth (1972) presented findings pertinent to the argument that the responsiveness of a mother figure to infant signals promotes the development of social competence. These findings emerged from a short-term longitudinal study of the development of the infant during the first year of life. The subjects were 29 infant-mother pairs from white middle class families of Baltimore (U.S.A.). They were observed in their own homes at intervals of three weeks, each visit lasting approximately four hours.

The signalling behaviour that concerned the investigators in this study was crying. Each instance of crying that occurred in the course of a home visit was coded. Aiming the particulars coded were the duration of the cry, whether the mother responded to it or ignored it, and, if she responded to it, how long she delayed before responding. Investigators were interested in ascertaining whether a mother's responsiveness was associated with a change in the incidence and duration of infant crying in the course of the first year of life. They were also interested in teasing out the direction of effects—a difficult matter in a naturalistic study.

The first step in the analysis was to examine the stability of infant crying throughout the first year and to compare it with the stability of maternal responsiveness to crying over the same period. Their findings suggested that there is no stability in infant crying until the very end of the first year, and therefore no support for the view that babies who cry more than others at the end of the first year do so because they are constitutionally irritable. The second step was to consider the intercorrelation between the number of crying episodes ignored by the mother and the frequency of infant crying episodes.

Even though crying may be age appropriate at the beginning of the first year, substantially diminished crying is appropriate towards the end of the first year and later. It is evident that maternal unresponsiveness to crying does not diminish it. On the contrary, it tends to prolong this form of signalling up to atleast the end of the first year. If, however, an infant's competence is viewed as depending on its mother's cooperativeness, one might argue that a one-year old child must be able to signal effectively if it is to be deemed competent.

This particular study gives credence to the importance of contingency established early in life. It implies that the responsiveness of mother helps to establish a contingency between infant's crying and mother's behaviour. The learning of the relationship gradually generalizes to other person's behaviour and events. As a result, this helps to foster a contingency between child's behaviour and outcomes not only in the physical world but also in interpersonal domain. The child develops a sense of mastering the physical world as well as strengthening interpersonal trust.

In a similar study, Skinner (1986) examined the relation between caregiver's contingent and sensitive behaviour and child's perceived control. In that study, 120 3.5 to 4.5 years old children and their mothers were taken for a problem solving task. In the task, mothers were instructed to help their children successfully execute six steps in the folding of an object. Interactions between the mother and the children were videotaped. Three kinds of mother behaviour namely sensitive responsiveness, sensitive initiation, and contingency were assessed. Four child behaviours (activity, active engagement, active non-engagement, child perceived control) were included in the analysis.

Analysis of the results was conducted in two steps. First, the interrelations amongst mothers' own behaviours and amongst children's behaviours were examined. Second, two strategies were used to explore the relationship between mothers' behaviour on the one hand and children's behaviour and perceived control on the other. The correlations among contingency, sensitive responsiveness, and sensitive initiation in three child contexts (child-off-the task, child-on-the task, and child-in-management) showed that mothers who showed sensitive initiation when the child was on task also showed sensitive initiation when management of the child's off task behaviour was required. Sensitive initiation in child management was also positively correlated with sensitive responsiveness. However, responsiveness was negatively correlated with sensitive initiation in giving the child overall task instructions. None of the child behaviours (active engagement, active non-engagement, independence) was interrelated. In addition, none of the behaviours was related to perceived control.

On the basis of relationship between mother's behaviour and child functioning, it was observed that a child's perceived control and child's activity were related to mother's sensitive initiation in child-in-task and child-in-management. But child's independence behaviour was strongly and negatively correlated with mother's sensitive responsiveness and more moderately negatively correlated with mother's sensitive initiation in child-in-task and child-in-management contexts.

On the whole, the study revealed that children's perceived control was closely related to mother's sensitive initiation. Mother's sensitive responsiveness, sensitive initiation and contingent behaviour were interrelated and correlated with child's active engagement in the problem solving task. Furthermore, mother's sensitive initiation and child's active engagement were reciprocal in that mother's sensitive initiation increased the probability of child's active engagement. Child's active engagement increased the probability of mother's sensitive initiation.

In a recent study, Hokoda and Finchman (1995) investigated origin of children's helplessness and mastery achievement patterns in the family. They observed third grade children and their mothers performing a series of solvable and unsolvable problem-solving-tasks. Mothers of mastery-oriented children showed sensitivity and responsiveness in their children's ability perception and requests for help. They also supported mastery behaviour of their children by increasing task-focused teaching behaviour and maintaining high positive affect during unsolvable puzzles. Moreover, in the face of failures, they retrained their children's low-ability attributions and performance goal statements, while performing task-oriented behaviour. These findings are consistent with Skinner's (1986) emphasis on the role of early contingent sensitive responsiveness of mothers in the context of ontogenesis of children's helplessness.

Parental Expectancy

The role of expectancy has amply been demonstrated in children's growth and development. Rosenthal and Jacobson (1968) have shown that teachers' high expectations regarding students' performance bring about 20-point IQ gains. Similarly, in the context of organizations; high expectations of managers regarding workers' skill is related to better performance of employees. This effect, known as *pygmalion effect*, is not confined to school and work setting. It is plausible that parents' high expectation mediate between parental socialization and children's competence. Parental expectation, being one of the important indicators of socialization, is likely to influence the development of children's helplessness.

There is considerable amount of cross-cultural literature to suggest that family functions as a "learning environment" and the cultural origin of the members of the family influences this learning environment (Kagitcibasi, 1996). Furthermore, there is evidence to show that cultural background influences parents' views about child-rearing practices (Lambert, Hamers & Frasure-Smith, 1979; Rosenthal & Bornholt, 1987), their interactions with children, especially the strategies they use to teach their children (Laosa, 1980) and their attitudes towards their children's temperaments (Pieri, Garino, Samson & Oberklaid, 1986). A number of studies have focused expectations that parents have regarding the development of different competencies in their children. It has been suggested that these expectations are mediated by, among other factors, the cultural settings in which children are reared. The values that are held to be important within a culture are likely to be reflected in the development theories held by parents of that culture. For example, it is reflected in their expectations about the time-tabling of developmental achievements in their children's lives. These studies, all of mothers, have shown that within a society, expectations vary as a function of cultural background (Goodnow, Cashmore, Cotton & Knight, 1984; Hess, Kashigawi, Azuma, Price & Dickson, 1980, Ninio, 1979).

Rosenthal and Bornholt's (1988) study of Greek and Anglo-Australian families indicated cultural variation. Expectations about the age in which certain competencies emerge were elicited from members (mother, father, adolescent) of families. They were asked to nominate describable qualities for teenagers and adults. The development timetable questionnaire included 65 items representing behaviours in eight domains. Every respondent was asked independently to decide the age at which a child would be expected to show the characteristic described by each item. The correspondence between the qualities regarded as important and those exempted in the developmental time-table questionnaire could be assessed. Preliminary analysis showed that there were no significant main effects of gender or ordinal position of the child, nor any significant interaction suggested that in Greco-Australian families young adolescents are expected to engage in unsupervised activity and to show greater self-control and respect at an earlier age than in Anglo-Australian families. The converse holds for responsibility, social behaviour with peers, interpersonal sensitivity, initiative and independence, and personal maturity.

With a view to examining the role of parental expectancy, Sahoo and Nanda (1988) carried out an empirical study involving mothers of mastery-oriented and the learned-helpless children in urban India. On the basis of a standardized measure of helplessness, children were classified into helpless and mastery categories. Subsequently the mothers of the mastery-oriented and helpless children were asked to indicate the age at which they expect their children to show some specific capabilities. These capabilities included seeing, hearing, babbling, identifying mother, identifying other persons, speaking, thinking, understanding words, crawling, sitting, walking, and identifying pictures. Mothers were also asked to indicate the age at which mothers extend certain specific care-giving activities. These activities included feeding by spoon, stopping breast feeding, weaning baby from bottle to cup, teaching baby not to touch fragile objects, letting baby start to feed himself/herself, starting toilet training, and start telling stories. It is obvious that a lower age level is indicative of high expectancy.

The comparison of mothers' expectancy revealed that mothers of mastery-oriented children had higher expectancy than mothers of helpless children. Although the higher expectancy of mothers of mastery-oriented children relative to expectancy of mothers of helpless children was not statistically significant in all areas of child's activity, the difference was marked in specific areas such as child's speaking, identifying picture of objects, and feeding by spoon. Sahoo and Sia (1988) conducted similar study in rural setting and found similar patterns that mothers of mastery oriented (MO) children demonstrate higher expectancy as compared to mothers of learned helpless children. These are consistent with the model of Learned Helplessness (LH). The experience of no-control is mediated by several factors. It is postulated that mother's expectancy is related to child's performance and his or her subsequent formation of adaptive (vis-à-vis maladaptive) orientation to achievements situation (Dweck & Licht, 1980).

TABLE 2.1: Mean and Standard Deviation of Expectancy Scores (Months at which Children are Expected to Demonstrate Activities) of Mothers of Learned-Helpless and Mastery-Oriented Children

Care giving activities	*Mothers of Learned Helpless Children*		*Mothers of Mastery-Oriented Children*		
	Mean	*SD*	*Mean*	*SD*	*t*
1. Feeding by spoon	5.23	5.93	2.22	2.20	2.07*
2. Stop breast feeding	23.75	15.12	18.74	10.74	1.30
3. Wean baby from bottle to cup	23.95	10.45	28.05	13.21	1.06
4. Teach baby not to touch fragile objects	34.42	16.61	26.83	15.79	1.44
5. Let the baby start to feed himself	38.70	15.59	36.66	14.05	4.42
6. Start toilet training	31.90	17.21	48.33	14.25	10.43
7. Start telling stories	44.74	14.26	40.24	13.00	1.01

Note: Lower number indicates higher expectancy.
* $p < .05$.

TABLE 2.2: Mean and Standard Deviation of Expectancy Scores (Months at which Children are Expected to be Capable of the following Activities) of Mothers of Learned-Helpless and Mastery-Oriented Children

Capabilities	*Mothers of Learned-Helpless Children*		*Mothers of Mastery-Oriented Children*		
	Mean	*SD*	*Mean*	*SD*	*t*
See	5.26	13.40	1.56	2.88	1.18
Hear	6.31	13.34	3.05	2.27	1.05
Identify his mother	4.74	4.03	4.11	3.53	0.52
Identify other persons	11.72	10.51	9.00	4.5	1.04
Think	44.05	29.01	41.13	23.68	0.34
Babble	13.78	7.14	12.40	6.58	0.62
Speak	25.73	10.22	19.22	7.14	2.35**
Understand words	30.26	22.39	31.76	17.86	0.23
Crawl	6.76	1.44	7.38	1.72	1.24
Sit	7.78	1.47	8.44	2.16	1.10
Walk	14.57	6.34	12.88	5.58	0.88
Identify pictures of objects	39.84	19.53	27.18	11.36	2.44*

Note: * $p < .05$.
** $p < .01$.

Sia and Sahoo (1991) attempted to cross-validate the role of expecting across urban and rural settings within the scope of a single investigation. The study showed consistent pattern of higher expectancy of urban mothers. With exception of telling stories, feeding by spoon, seeing, hearing, speaking and understanding words, urban mothers indicated a lower age at which a number activities are supposed to emerge. The subcultural differences suggested significant role of cultural and environmental setting.

TABLE 2.3: Mean Expectancy Score (in Months) of Mothers for Capabilities of their Children

Capacities	*Orientation*	*Setting*		
		Rural	*Urban*	*Combined*
(1)	(2)	(3)	(4)	(5)
To see	Mothers of L.H.	0.0	5.00	2.50
	Mothers of M.O.	0.04	0.85	0.45
	Combined	0.02	2.93	
To hear	Mothers of L.H.	2.47	6.70	4.59
	Mothers of M.O.	2.86	2.80	2.83
	Combined	2.66	4.75	
To identify mother	Mothers of L.H.	6.22	4.65	5.43
	Mothers of M.O.	6.56	3.75	5.15
	Combined	6.39	4.20	
To identify other persons	Mothers of L.H.	8.87	10.10	9.98
	Mothers of M.O.	15.26	8.25	11.76
	Combined	12.57	9.17	
To think	Mothers of L.H.	69.48	41.85	55.66
	Mothers of M.O.	42.08	31.12	33.60
	Combined	55.78	36.48	
To babble	Mothers of L.H.	11.04	13.10	12.07
	Mothers of M.O.	12.34	10.65	11.49
	Combined	11.69	11.87	
To speak	Mothers of L.H.	17.30	24.45	20.87
	Mothers of M.O.	17.82	17.85	17.83
	Combined	17.56	21.15	
To understand words	Mothers of L.H.	23.83	28.75	26.29
	Mothers of M.O.	26.00	27.55	26.77
	Combined	24.92	28.15	
To crawl	Mothers of L.H.	8.95	6.76	7.86
	Mothers of M.O.	9.47	7.32	8.39
	Combined	9.21	7.04	
To sit	Mothers of L.H.	8.57	7.40	7.98
	Mothers of M.O.	11.30	8.05	9.68
	Combined	9.94	7.73	

(*Contd.*)

TABLE 2.3 (*Contd.*)

(1)	(2)	(3)	(4)	(5)
To walk	Mothers of L.H.	15.00	13.85	14.43
	Mothers of M.O.	15.56	12.21	13.89
	Combined	15.28	13.03	
To identify pictures	Mothers of L.H.	33.87	37.85	35.86
	Mothers of M.O.	36.95	24.00	30.47
	Combined	35.41	30.93	
General observation	Mothers of L.H.	16.53	17.18	16.85
	Mothers of M.O.	16.64	12.88	14.76
	Combined	16.59	15.03	

Note: Lower number indicates higher expectancy.

TABLE 2.4: Mean Expectancy Scores (in Months) of Mothers for Care-Giving Activities Towards their Children

Care Giving Activities	*Orientation*	*Setting*		
		Rural	*Urban*	*Combined*
Feeding by spoon	Mothers of L.H.	2.74	5.35	4.05
	Mothers of M.O.	1.91	2.00	1.95
	Combined	2.33	3.67	
Stopping breast feeding	Mothers of L.H.	31.13	23.75	27.44
	Mothers of M.O.	29.73	16.10	22.92
	Combined	30.43	19.93	
Weaning baby from bottle to cup	Mothers of L.H.	24.52	23.95	24.24
	Mothers of M.O.	30.52	21.10	25.81
	Combined	27.52	22.53	
Teaching baby not to touch fragile objects	Mothers of L.H.	29.39	32.70	31.05
	Mothers of M.O.	34.17	24.70	29.44
	Combined	31.78	28.70	
Letting baby start to feed himself/herself	Mothers of L.H.	39.65	38.70	39.17
	Mothers of M.O.	33.65	32.70	33.17
	Combined	36.65	35.70	
Starting toilet training	Mothers of L.H.	54.52	51.90	53.21
	Mothers of M.O.	53.21	46.50	49.85
	Combined	53.87	49.20	
Starting telling stories	Mothers of L.H.	18.78	44.74	31.76
	Mothers of M.O.	19.82	35.70	27.76
	Combined	19.30	40.22	
General observation	Mothers of L.H.	29.02	31.24	30.13
	Mothers of M.O.	27.71	24.27	25.99
	Combined	28.37	27.75	

Note: Lower number indicates higher expectancy.

In a later study (Sia, Sahoo & Sia, 1998), expectancy of mothers and fathers has been compared. The procedure was similar. It was shown that mothers of MO children indicated higher expectancy, especially in the areas of physical activity. Fathers, on the other hand, demonstrated higher expectancy for cognitive (thinking and coping) activities. The study also examined parental expectancy with respect to children's adaptation in home and school settings. A number of coping activities were indicated and parents were asked to indicate the age at which their children are expected to initiate these coping activities. The activities included working with others, inviting friends, visiting friends' houses, playing together, being respectful to others, consulting teachers regarding assignment, working independently in absence of teachers, and discussing lessons with others. The results indicated significant role of orientation on parental expectancy with respect to children's coping abilities like working together, visiting friends' houses, and being respectful to others. As shown by Table 2.5, parents of MO children reveal higher expectancy than do parents of LH children. Furthermore, it was shown that fathers indicate higher expectancy for these coping activities of their children than do mothers.

TABLE 2.5: Mean Expectancy Scores of Parents of Helpless and Mastery-Oriented Children for Coping Activities

Coping items	*Orientation of children*	*Parents of boys*	*Parents of girls*	*All parents*
(1)	(2)	(3)	(4)	(5)
Working together	L.H.	114.00	183.36	148.68
	M.O.	84.27	157.63	120.95
	Combined	99.13	170.49	—
Inviting friends	L.H.	83.45	131.73	107.59
	M.O.	76.91	129.27	103.09
	Combined	80.81	130.50	—
Visiting friend's home	L.H.	87.47	134.00	110.73
	M.O.	77.72	133.91	105.81
	Combined	82.59	133.95	—
Playing together	L.H.	70.36	95.45	82.90
	M.O.	60.54	106.36	83.45
	Combined	65.45	100.91	—
Showing respect	L.H.	56.18	63.54	59.86
	M.O.	47.72	66.27	56.99
	Combined	51.95	64.90	—
Consulting teachers on assignment	L.H.	123.54	171.82	147.68
	M.O.	109.63	152.18	130.90
	Combined	116.58	162.00	—
Being engaged in the absence of teachers	L.H.	104.18	127.36	115.77
	M.O.	93.00	125.18	109.09
	Combined	98.59	126.27	—

(*Contd.*)

TABLE 2.5 (*Contd.*)

(1)	(2)	(3)	(4)	(5)
Discussing lessons	L.H.	157.09	200.82	178.95
	M.O.	128.45	180.27	154.36
	Combined	142.77	190.54	—
Total coping ratings	L.H.	790.86	1105.56	948.21
	M.O.	663.72	1054.31	661.52
	Combined	727.29	1082.43	—

Note: Lower number indicates higher expectancy.

In sum, there seems to be a pattern relating to the role of parental expectancy. Higher expectancies play a positive role in promoting children's competence. There could be several plausible explanations for this pygmalion effect. It is likely that parental expectancy influences the quality of parent-child interaction. Parents with higher expectancies are likely to behave in a more positive manner and children are likely to behave in ways that would confirm parental expectations.

Apart from the expectancy of caregivers, attitudinal emphases constitute important elements of socialization.

Attitudinal Emphases

Parental attitudes have been recognized as a central component of socialization process. The attitudes and values parents carry explicitly or implicitly are mediated to their children through instructions, reward and punishment systems, and other techniques (Whiting, 1981). Although there are not many studies to examine the relationship between parental socialization and children's helplessness, some conjectures are derived from the literature on achievement motivation and psychological differentiation. Winterbottom (1958) has clearly shown that individual's need for achievement is linked to childhood training for independence. McClelland (1961) has emphasized this maternal training for child's independence as an antecedent of achievement. Similarly, Witkin and Berry (1975) have identified the role of masterly training in the development of children's psychological differentiation.

The human infants are perhaps the most profoundly dependent living organisms; they depend upon the care of others for their survival. They have only a few reflexes and physiological processes essential to life. At the same time, human infants are endowed with the great potential for the development of personal adequacy and effectiveness.

Sullivan (1953) stresses the crucial importance of the quality of mother's emotional reaction to her baby's needs both physical and emotional. The two factors of importance in determining the general nature of mother-infant interactions are, of course, the baby's temperamental nature and the mother's sensitivity and responsiveness (Skinner, 1986) to his or her basic needs. The nature of the baby's most frequent and prevailing effective experiences in relation to the mother's care can thus range from feelings of anxiety and distress to feelings of security, comfort and "trust" in response to the mother's "tenderness."

Actually there is relatively little research evidence as to the relation between the kind of mothering young infants receive and their development (Yarrow, 1961). However, Caldwell *et al.* (1963) have shown that one-year old infants who had been cared for by their own mothers only were more active, more emotionally dependent on their mothers, and more emotional in their interaction with their mothers than were infants of the same age who had experienced "polymaternal" care.

As the children's manipulative and locomotor capacities develop, the child's drive to explore and perceive more and more of their environment becomes a dominant factor in their behavioural and emotional development. As they explore the objects of their environment and grasp and manipulate the objects in space, they grow in their awareness of the relation of their own acts to the objects about them. With this achievement of independence and competence, the dependable ones are no longer completely dominated by the care-givers' demands. The parents and care-givers, on the contrary, begin now to be more restrictive and even punitive. This concern of the care-givers and their interference with children's freedom makes children more aware of these functions and the frustrations and gratifications associated with autonomy. The children thus become more preoccupied with freedom in relation to their growing sense of autonomy.

These environmental trends, however, do not function evenly for all children, because of certain selective environmental factors (Whiting, 1981) and specific qualities of parental interaction. There is a great variation in mother's personality make-up and in their beliefs regarding socialization. Similarly, the variation in cultural (or subcultural) norms bring limiting and amplifying conditions for development of certain traits. There is a growing body of literature in anthropology and psychology with respect to the role of parental attitude towards socialization. Whiting and Child's (1953) work and Whiting, Child,

Lambert and Whiting's (1963) six-nation-study amply demonstrate the significance of socialization emphases.

In the context of the development of children's helplessness, there are no empirical studies. However, Sia and Sahoo's (1991) study that looked into mother's expectancy also investigated the role of socialization parameters. The socialization questionnaire was specifically developed to suit socio-cultural settings of eastern India prior to the final use of this scale. The development and validation of the measure indicated three factors: independence-autonomy, positive consequences of autonomy, and acceptability of the helpless child. These factors were derived on the basis of the factor analysis. Independence-autonomy factor pertains to beliefs regarding the child's independent and autonomous activity. Positive consequences refer to the perception of benefits (outcomes) of granting autonomy to the child. The acceptability factor relates to the degree of tolerating the child who is helpless.

As described earlier, mothers of mastery-oriented (MO) and learned helpless (LH) children were compared with respect to their socialization emphases. It was shown that mothers of MO children indicated greater emphasis on independence-autonomy and perceived more positive consequences of autonomy than did mothers of LH children. However, there was no difference between groups with respect to the acceptability factor. Furthermore, urban mothers indicated greater emphasis on independence-autonomy, positive consequences of autonomy, and acceptability of the helpless child than did rural mothers. The findings with respect to mothers of MO children vis-à-vis mothers of LH children were in the predicted pattern. In addition, the urban-rural difference brought out a very important factor—subcultural difference in a plural society.

TABLE 2.6: Mean Scores on Various Socialization Indices

Socialization Domains	*Socialization Indices*	*Orientation of Children*	*Setting*		
			Rural	*Urban*	*Combined*
Parents' attitude towards child rearing	Autonomy and independence	L.H.	2.96	3.66	3.31
		M.O.	3.04	3.98	3.51
		All participants	3.00	3.82	
	Perception of positive consequences	L.H.	2.03	2.31	2.17
		M.O.	2.20	2.41	2.44
		All participants	3.02	3.63	
	Acceptability	L.H.	3.02	3.63	3.33
		M.O.	3.08	3.57	3.33
		All participants	3.05	3.60	

Recently several authors have stressed and evaluated the nature of parent-child interaction on the basis of parental attitude (Moss & Jones, 1977, Parke, Hymel, Power Tinsly, 1980). According to Parke (1978), parental beliefs and attitudes are regarded as filters, through which the behaviour of children is processed. Parental attitudes play an important role in the way in which parents and children mutually regulate each other.

Rearing Strategies

The role of child rearing practices is more direct compared to altitudinal emphasis. A number of anthropologists and psychologists working in the tradition of culture and personality have emphasized child rearing as factors in personality development (Whiting, 1981; Whiting & Whiting, 1975). Even in recent years a growing body of evidence suggests the relationship between child rearing and adult personality (Kagitcibasi, 1996).

Das (1989) intended to map the child rearing practices mothers adopt in India. The study adopted a 2 (learned-helpless versus mastery-oriented) × 2 (child's sex) ×2 (urban and rural setting) factorial design. Child rearing measures consisted of four dimensions: achievement-oriented, responsibility-oriented, dependency-oriented rearing, and leniency in punishment. Mothers of MO children and LH children were asked to indicate the frequency with which they adopt a rearing option. Different behaviour options were expressed in form of different statements.

While no significant difference was shown across mothers of MO and LH children with respect to achievement, dependency and leniency, mothers of MO children indicated greater responsibility-oriented rearing than did mothers of LH children. It is plausible that mothers' assignment of responsibility to their children offers opportunity of successful performance on the part of children. This experience of effortfulness and success fosters competence in them. On the contrary, mothers who do not offer responsibility training to children tend to inhibit the growth of competence by restricting their children's opportunity to learn the value of effortfulness. The learning experiences associated with task performance have been identified as correlates of child's motivation (Dweck, 1986).

Furthermore, responsibility-oriented rearing also induces training for self-control. When children are assigned tasks such as taking care of siblings, the successful completion of the task requires an adequate management of their emotion. Mothers who provide such opportunity tend to induce self-control in their children. The management of affect has been shown to be a correlate of learned resourcefulness, a process that runs counter to helplessness (Rosenbaum & Ben-Ari, 1985).

With respect to responsibility training given to boys vis-à-vis girls, no difference was found, Although Barry, Bacon and Child (1957) report that responsibility training is stronger for girls than for boys, the investigators also report cases where a more formal or systematic training for boys seem to imply greater pressure on them towards responsibility. In Indian socio-cultural system, two different types of role performance seem to generate similar pressures for responsibility training. While responsibility training given to boys is geared to prepare them for economic role, there is also pressure for responsibility training in the direction of preparing girls for multiple social roles. Thus, the absence of sex difference is consistent with the sex role socialization in India.

Paikray and Sahoo (1994) designed a study to examine the issue in mother-child interaction contexts. They developed and validated a parental Interactional Style Questionnaire. The factor analytic study identified nine specific styles of interaction. *Authoritarian* style is denoted by elements to shape, control, and evaluate the behaviour of the child according to a set standard of conduct. Such parents value obedience and favour punitive, forceful measures to curb behaviour they think is wrong. When such parents show rejecting attitudes, their style is described as *authoritarian rejecting*. The *authoritative* style defines parental direction of the child's activities in a rational and issue-oriented manner. These parents encourage verbal give-and-take; the child is given reason for policy. Although control is exercised by these parents, the child is not hemmed with restrictions. The *permissive* pattern attempts to behave non-punitively and in accepting and affirmative way towards the child. The parents avoid control on the child and the child is allowed to regulate his or her behaviour. The *rejecting-neglecting* pattern is characterized by minimal encouragement of independence and by failure to enrich the child's environment. These parents also discourage emotional support. The *harmonious* pattern is denoted by quality of harmony at home. These parents are non-conforming. They encourage independence and provide a very enriched environment. Harmonious families are characterized as having control but not as exercising control. *Indulgent-protective* parents demonstrate a pattern emphasizing emotional dependency of their children. These parents show unnecessary expression of care and do not allow their children to experiment and to mistake. *Appeasing* pattern defines an approach which is predominantly conciliatory. These parents tend to avoid issues and try to circumvent problems that arise *Temporizing* style is indicative of vascillating approach. It does not follow any consistent pattern. Confusion characterizes this style.

Mothers of mastery-oriented and mothers of learned helpless children were compared on each of these dimensions. The parental Interactional Style Questionnaire required these mothers to indicate the frequency with which they use each form of interaction. Each of the interactional style was represented by several statements. Sahoo and Paikray's (1994) study indicated that mothers of learned helpless children adopt authoritarian-rejecting, rejecting-neglecting, and temporizing interaction styles to a greater extent than do mothers of mastery-oriented children. On the contrary, mothers of mastery-oriented children indicate greater authoritative and permissive interaction styles compared with mothers of helpless children.

It is plausible that mothers using authoritarian-rejecting and rejecting-neglecting pattern do not feel concerned about child's activities. They do not take interest in child's activities; rather they put down child's effortfulness in an authoritarian manner. The lowering of guidance, encouragement and appreciation induces in the child a sense of helplessness. It was also found that mothers of LH children used temporizing interactional strategy. As indicated earlier, temporizing pattern denotes the lack of consistency. Mothers adopting temporizing style do not employ any consistent principle but they are dominated by the fluctuations of situations. It is obvious that such mothers prevent their children from forming appropriate connections between events and outcomes. Thus, the tendency of mothers to use authoritarian-rejecting, rejecting-neglecting, and temporizing rearing strategies appears to be a logical antecedent of children's helplessness.

On the contrary, mothers of MO children were found to employ authoritative and permissive styles to a greater extent compared with mothers of LH children. It is postulated that mothers of MO children use authoritative rearing strategies in order to retain control over their children with respect to certain important activities of their children. But they do not put unnecessary restrictions in the areas of other activities of their children. This explains the fact that mothers of MO children are more permissive, although authoritative. In other words, mothers of MO children do exercise authoritative influence in some key activity domains of their children while they use permissive styles with respect to less critical areas of children's activity.

Sahoo and Paikray (1994) also looked into the target of socialization. The pattern of interaction as directed towards boys vis-à-vis girls was examined. It was shown that mothers used authoritative and permissive interactional style more often for boys than for girls. The reasons that prompt mothers to adopt such rearing styles are conceivable. It is observed that mothers depend on their sons to a greater extent than do they depend on their daughters for economic security in India. The welfare system operative in the family setting is centered on sons (boys). Consequently, parents tend to retain some control over the activities of their sons so that the chances of their future settlement are not dampened. This tendency on the part of parents persuades them to adopt authoritative interactional styles towards boys. For similar reasons, they do not treat girls as supporter of their economic well-being and they become less authoritative with girls.

While the economic motives of mothers are likely to induce authoritative interactional style for boys, social motive prompt them to adopt less permissive style for girls than for boys. In traditional and transitional communities of India, girls are considered susceptible to social criticisms when they deviate from social norms and standards. On the contrary, boys do not receive similar amount of criticism when they show violation of same magnitude. As a result, parents are less permissive with girls than are they when dealing with boys.

Although the study provides some important clues regarding the role of rearing strategies, the question of parent-child perceptual congruency remains unanswered. Does the child perceive an interactional style the way a parent perceives? Is interactional style, as perceived by the child, linked to helplessness?

In a later study, Sahoo and Kar (1996) compared MO and LH children with respect to their perception of parental interactional style. The parental Interactional Style Questionnaire indicated in Sahoo and Paikray's study was used. The MO and LH children did not differ with respect to their perception of eight styles, striking difference was noted on rejecting-neglecting interactional style. Learned helpless children perceived their parents to be more rejecting-neglecting than did MO children. This corroborated the previous study of Sahoo and Paikray (1994).

TABLE 2.7: Mean Scores of Children's Perception of Mothers' Interactional Styles

Interactional Styles	*MO Children*			*LH Children*		
	Boys	*Girls*	*All*	*Boys*	*Girls*	*All*
Authoritarian rejecting	11.99	11.81	11.90	12.13	12.49	12.31
Authoritarian not rejecting	12.84	12.97	12.91	12.40	13.18	12.69
Authoritative	15.86	16.59	16.23	15.78	16.52	16.11
Permissive	14.45	14.86	14.66	15.94	15.33	15.64
Rejecting neglecting	7.33	6.17	6.75	7.85	7.91	7.88
Harmonious	13.44	13.71	13.58	12.69	14.20	13.45
Indulgent protective	17.83	17.89	17.98	18.00	18.55	18.02
Appeasing	7.16	7.15	7.16	8.79	7.66	8.22
Temporizing	12.42	12.64	12.53	13.53	12.94	13.24

Note: Number of items for each style is not same. Hence the maximum mean scores is different for different Interactional styles.

TABLE 2.8: Mean Scores of Children's Perception of Fathers' Interactional Styles

Interactional Styles	*MO Children*			*LH Children*		
	Boys	*Girls*	*All*	*Boys*	*Girls*	*All*
Authoritarian-rejecting	13.46	11.51	12.49	14.48	11.52	12.99
Authoritarian-not-rejecting	13.07	12.63	12.85	14.06	11.88	12.97
Authoritative	16.27	16.52	16.40	15.69	16.20	15.95
Permissive	14.91	14.24	14.57	14.89	14.62	14.76
Rejecting neglecting	7.33	6.12	6.73	8.89	6.88	7.89
Harmonious	13.90	14.43	14.17	13.91	14.53	14.22
Indulgent protective	18.04	17.06	17.55	18.64	17.04	17.84
Appeasing	7.69	6.94	7.32	8.60	7.04	7.82
Temporizing	14.10	12.40	13.26	14.69	12.03	13.36

Note: Number of items for each style is not same. Hence the maximum mean scores is different for different Interactional styles.

As indicated earlier, rejecting-neglecting behaviour denotes highly controlling and authoritarian behaviour of the parents towards their children. In rejecting-neglecting behaviour, parents reject their children's every activity and cannot recognize their ideas and opinions. Their child-rearing practices are negative in nature. They cannot encourage their children to be independent and do not provide them the enriched environmental inputs through which the proper behavioural development of the child can be stimulated. Parents do not provide rewards contingent on the behaviour. It is also likely that parental rigidity and negativism prevent them to provide rewards contingent on children's behaviour. Whenever parents' rewards are offered, they appear to be unrelated to children's desired activity. So the child encounters a non-contingent environment at home. The children of such parents fail to associate between events and outcomes. The repeated exposure to such familial non-contingent atmosphere is likely to induce helplessness.

On the contrary, it can be conjectured that reward contingency develops in case of MO children. In case of MO children, a lower degree of rejecting-neglecting implies a careful match between parental words and deeds. They associate between their actions and outcomes. They are reinforced by their parents for desirable behaviour. So their actions quickly, consistently and discriminately lead to formation of cognitive associations. In this way, reward contingency aids MO children to be competent.

Furthermore, the findings of the study indicated that LH children perceived their mothers' appeasing behaviour to a greater extent than did MO children. The approach of the appeasing mothers is predominated by a tendency to avoid conflict with the child. These mothers tend to avoid issues and to circumvent problems that arise. Hence appeasing mothers do not impart responsibility training to their children. From empirical research, it is shown that mothers of mastery-oriented children use responsibility training more often than mothers of LH children (Das, 1989).

The examination of perception of boys vis-à-vis girls showed some interesting features. Although LH children perceived their mothers (not fathers) as more appeasing than did MO children, a significant difference was noted with respect to boys' perception of their fathers. Boys perceived their fathers more appeasing than did girls.

As pointed out earlier, LH children perceived their parents (both father and mother) more rejecting-neglecting than did MO children. Yet, further examination showed that boys not only considered their fathers more rejecting-neglecting they also perceived their fathers more authoritarian (both authoritarian-rejecting and authoritarian-not-rejecting), indulgent protective, and temporizing than did girls. However, girls perceived their mothers more harmonious than did boys.

In general, boys more often than girls perceive their fathers to use authoritarian-rejecting, authoritarian-not-rejecting, rejecting-neglecting, indulgent-protective, appeasing, and temporizing behaviour. Such differential perception of fathers on the part of boys seems to have a cultural explanation. In Indian socio-cultural system, much preferences are given to the male child. Indian parents value male child because of the possibility of economic security during problematic days of their old age. It appears that fathers' over-eagerness to mould the child according to a set of standards of conduct prompt them to use authoritarian-rejecting and authoritarian-not-rejecting behaviour towards their boys. Due to higher expectancy from boys, fathers are likely to be impatient and express authoritarian behaviour.

The study also deepens the impression that fathers seem to be confused about making decisions for their sons. On the one hand, their eagerness to mould sons' future make them authoritarian. On the other hand, they become indulgent-prefective in trying to insulate their boys. The lack of clear decision prevents them from being consistent with respect to rearing of their boys. As a result, they also adopt temporizing and appeasing interactional styles.

An important aspect of this line of investigation is the consideration of congruency between parental reporting and children's perception. Although Sahoo and Kar (1996) reported only a moderate congruency between parents' and children's perception, there is a fair amount of correspondence between findings based on parental reports (Das, 1989; Sahoo & Paikray, 1994) and results obtained from children's ratings (Sahoo & Kar, 1996). The role of rejecting-neglecting style evinced by Sahoo and Kar's (1996) study implicitly admits the adverse effects of the lack of concern (Sahoo & Paikray, 1994) and lack of responsibility training (Das, 1989). In sum, the absence of a consistent parent-child bonding seems to underlie the child's helplessness.

Attribution Training

It has been posited that helplessness is significantly linked to insidious attributions for explaining bad events in terms of internality, globality, and stability. A large body of empirical studies have demonstrated the association between children's helplessness and their internal, global and stable explanatory styles (Nolen-Hoeksema, Girgus & Seligman, 1986). Further evidence suggests that children's attributional styles remain stable over time (Fincham, Diener & Hokoda, 1987; Joiner & Wagner, 1995).

Since composite attributional style for bad events has been regarded as a risk factors in the development of helplessness as well as depression (Peterson & Seligman, 1983), an important issue concerns the question whether parents transmit their insidious attributional styles to their children. Seligman *et al.* (1984) collected attributional style scores of parents and their children as well as their depression inventory scores. Children whose parents completed questionnaires did not differ from the other children with respect to attribution or depression. It was shown that mothers' composite style for bad events correlated with her child's composite score for bad events ($r = .39$, $p < .01$) and with her child's depression scores ($r = .42$, $p < .005$). It was also indicated that mother's depressive symptoms correlated with her child's depressive symptoms ($r = .37$, $p < .01$). However, father's attributional style and depression were not related to scores of his mate and their child. The examination of intercorrelations between scores of mother and child suggested that the relationship mainly resulted from the contributions of the internality and globality dimensions.

Sahoo and Paikray (1994) compared attributional styles of mothers of helpless and competent children. They used a Projective Inventory of Helplessness and Attribution. The test presents a couple of stories culled from day-to-day life. Each story is followed by a number of statements relating to the events and characters depicted in the story. Respondents are asked to indicate their agreement and disagreement with each of the statements. A scoring key exists to determine respondent's scores on helplessness as well as internal, global and stable attributions. A similar Projective Inventory of Helplessness and Attribution also exists for adult respondents. The investigators categorized children into mastery-oriented and helpless on the basis of test scores. The comparison of MO and LH children clearly showed that LH children indicate internal, global and stable attributions for explaining bad events. When mothers of these two groups were compared on attribution, significant difference was indicated only on global attribution style.

Sahoo and Sia (1990) also examined the difference between parents of MO and LH children with respect to attribution styles. Both fathers and mothers of LH children showed greater internality, stability and globality than did parents of MO children. However, the comparison between father and mother showed that father offered training for internal attribution more than did mothers, whereas mothers offered training for globality more than did fathers.

TABLE 2.9: Mean Negative Attribution Scores of Parents of Mastery-Oriented and Learned Helpless Children

Attribution	*Parents of MO Children*			*Parents of LH Children*		
	Father	*Mother*	*Combined*	*Father*	*Mother*	*Combined*
Internality	45.77	48.02	46.90	80.52	48.84	49.88
Stability	23.66	21.88	22.27	77.18	72.45	74.82
Globality	24.86	25.02	25.44	68.93	70.20	69.62
Composite attribution	94.53	95.93	95.23	198.48	191.50	194.84

Thus, there is some evidence to suggest the relationship between parental attributional style and their children's style. Like the intrapsychic vicious circle of the depressives (Beck, 1967), helplessness and attributions may be embedded in an interpersonal vicious circle. The child may learn attributional styles from parents and these may then maintain each other. The child may influence the parents as much as the parents influence the child.

It is observed that children's composite negative attribution scores are related only to mothers' scores in western setting but linkage between parental attribution and children's attribution is indicated in Indian setting. It is plausible that fathers do not spend as much time with their children in west as they do spend in eastern countries.

The mechanisms by which parents and children converge on attributional style is a matter of conjecture. Kelley's attribution theory proposes that attributions result from the abstraction of causal relationships from actual events. Thus, the reasons children and parents have similar explanatory styles may be common experiences.

Parental Stress

The role of parental stress in inducing helplessness in children is a researchable topic. Of the various explanations proposed to account for the phenomenon of learned helplessness, one in particular involves the role of stress.

There is some experimental evidence to indicate that stress interferes with learning in laboratory animals. Altener, Kay, and Richter (1977) found that rats subjected to underwater experiences performed less well than control rats in the acquisition of escape avoidance. Weiss, Glazer and Poboresky (1976) found that animals subjected to cold swim treatment subsequently failed to learn avoidance. Biochemical examination revealed the animals had depleted noradrenergic neurochemicals in the brain. Accordingly reduced motor activity was postulated as the explanation of poor learning.

Of course, the question whether or not stress interferes with learning and exacerbates the learned helplessness phenomenon is linked with the type of stressor and the deficiency of task (Cotton & Smith, 1990). Cotton and Smith's observation fits well with current conceptualization of anxiety. It is known that moderate to high levels of anxiety improves performance on simple task, whereas moderate to high levels of anxiety has adverse effects on the performance of a complex task. Anxiety, as a drive, energizes all the habits that are evoked in a situation, both correct and incorrect. Higher level of anxiety tends to increase the absolute difference between the tendencies to respond correctly and incorrectly, compared with lower levels, to the detriment of correct responses. It follows logically that highly anxious individuals will perform worse than less anxious ones in complex learning situations. In other words, severe stressors (such as electric shock) would not only impair acquisition, it would also exacerbate helplessness deficits.

While there are a few animal experiments to demonstrate this role of stressors on learned helplessness (Smith, Wills & Naylor, 1981), there are no studies employing human subjects. However, a few researchers have examined the role of parental self-perception. For example, Sahoo and Das (1989) compared self-perception of mothers of MO and LH children. It was assumed that the development of child's self is influenced by mother's self-concepts. Without awareness and explicit training, mothers transmit their self-concepts to their children. However, it is also recognized that these transmissions interact with a variety of other extraneous influences stemming from peers, teachers and other important figures in child's life. But significance of parental self-concepts in general and mother's self-concept in particular seems to be crucial.

Although Sahoo and Das (1989) did adopt an elaborate measuring instrument for comparing mothers of MO and LH children, two factors (self-assurance and self-realization) were represented. Self-assurance refers to the degree of poise and confidence a parent exhibits while handling problems arising out of child management situations. Self-realization refers to the degree of personal satisfaction resulting from the happy and smooth relationship with children, spouse, neighbours and other important persons. These two parameters were chosen on the basis of the review of literature on Witken's concept of psychological differentiation. The studies of psychological differentiation analyze interaction-inhibiting and interaction-fostering factors, these studies show that mothers who are self-assured, self-realized are successful in fostering autonomous strivings in children.

It is expected that a mother who has herself achieved a sense of self-realization would be better able to permit her child to separate from her and to develop as an individual than a mother who lacks it. It is also expected that mothers who are self-assured would have less hesitation about setting and maintaining limits for their children, and so help them develop impulse-control. Mothers who lack self-assurance may be inconsistent and wavering at this fail to give support to a child's development of controls.

Apart from these considerations, there are a few other reasons for emphasizing self-assurance and self-realization. Complaints of being tired, worn-out, tense and nervous, and feeling unable to cope with family situations or problems in every-day living entered into judging a mother as self-realized. Predominantly complaining attitudes about the children were considered evidence of a lack, of self-realization. Complaints of both material and emotional deprivation and neglect by husbands provided further indicators of a lack of self-realization, although it was not known whether such complaints were based on facts. Complaints that father and son were aligned against the mother were also considered indicative of a lack of self-realization. Some mothers reported that the relation between father and son had left them out and made them feel "unloved". Lack of self-realization was also indicated when a mother stated that absence of practical assistance and emotional support from her husband in training up the children had created burdens she did not feel adequate to assume. The manner in which a mother resolved her conflict with her husband about child care provided evidence for judging both her self-realization and self-assurance. Das and Sahoo considered it suggestive of a lack of self-assurance in child rearing if a mother searched for and sought to elicit rules for child care from "the books", physicians or theories in vogue, among neighbours or friends, and yet derived little comfort or security from the advice she obtained.

Sahoo and Das (1989) study clearly showed greater self-assurance and self-realization of mothers of MO children as compared to mother of LH children. These findings are also supported by Sahoo and Nanda (1988) and Sia and Sahoo (1991). Sahoo and Sia adopted similar design and compared self-assurance and self-realization of parents of MO children and LH children. The observations were further strengthened.

TABLE 2.10: Mean Self-Assurance and Self-Realization Scores of Parents of Master-Oriented and Learned Helpless Children

Dimensions	*Parents of MO Children*			*Parents of LH Children*		
	Father	*Mother*	*Parents*	*Father*	*Mother*	*Parents*
Self-Assurance	48.23	48.75	48.49	22.88	23.25	23.06
Self-Realization	34.66	33.66	34.15	15.40	14.97	16.19

The significance of parental positive self-concept in general and maternal self-esteem in particular are believed to be relatively stable evaluative dispositions towards self. Although researchers now think of self-esteem such as self-power and self-worth, these aspects seem to be of varying weightage in different contexts. While the empirical studies reviewed in the context of development of children's helplessness have not included all aspects of parental self-evaluations, the positive role of self-assurance and self-realization in competence-inducing and helplessness-reducing situations offer workable solutions for child management programme.

3

EXPERIENTIAL ANTECEDENTS

The development of learned helplessness appears to be a product of both predisposing and precipitating factors. Although familial factors such as early contingency, parental attitudes, rearing strategies and attribution training are related to the insidious perception of no-control and maladaptive explanatory styles, they may not provide conditions strong enough for helplessness deficits to surface. However, the differential exposure to non-contingency seems to trigger off learned helplessness. This hypothesis predicts that those with a history of failure (e.g., the mentally retarded and learning disabled) would experience greater deficits than those with no history of failures. It also predicts that noncontingent mobiles would be detrimental to infant's development (Watson, 1977). Johnson (1981) provided some data relevant to this hypothesis. She found that failing students in a regular class persisted the least on an unsolvable puzzle when compared to average students in a regular class. While such studies suggest the predisposing role of early (distal) factors, the significance of more contemporaneous (proximal) experiential factors appear to precipitate the phenomenon of learned helplessness.

Performance Feedback

A plausible hypothesis explaining the development of learned helplessness in children involves differential exposure to performance feedback. Dweck, Davidson, Nelson and Enna (1978) contend that because of differential performance feedback in the classroom, girls are more likely than boys to attribute failure to lack of ability and become helpless. They observed teachers' evaluative feedback in fourth and fifth-grade classrooms and found that while boys and girls receive equal amount of negative feedback for the intellectual quality of their work, boys are, in addition, criticized just as often for non-intellectual aspects of their work (e.g., messiness). These feedback patterns when reproduced in a laboratory task showed that the girls' feedback pattern led both male and female subjects to attribute failure on a subsequence task to lack of ability. When subjects received the feedback characteristically given to boys, they attributed their failure to lack of effort or to the fussiness of evaluator. Thus, it is not the absolute frequency with which children experience criticism of their intellectual performance, but rather the relative frequencies of intellectual criticism to other types of criticism which may determine children's tendency to make effort attributions for failure.

The arguments can be extended further. If girls attribute failure to stable factors such as ability, they are likely to generalize low expectations for success to new situations. In contrast, if boys attribute failure to unstable factors, they are likely to expect their level of success to improve whenever they enter a new situation. This prediction received some support in the laboratory as boys' expectations recovered more than girls' when either the experimenter alone or both the experimenters and the task were changed (Dweck, Goetz, & Strauss, 1980). Dweck *et al.* extended the study to classroom situations and they also found that boys predicted significantly higher school examination grades than girls before receiving the first progress card of the school session. Even though boys has had actually received poorer grades at the end of the previous year, they did not generalize their performance expectations to the new classroom.

An interesting aspect of this hypothesis prompts one to determine whether similar feedback patterns occur in the family. Sahoo and Sia (1990) compared both fathers and mothers on the endorsement of internal (e.g., ability) versus external (e.g., effortfulness) statements they make when they come across success/failure of their sons/daughters. The analysis of result did not suggest differential pattern of feedback they direct toward their boys vis-à-vis girls.

Peer Influence

The place of a child in peer network has been linked to the child's learned helplessness. A number of studies have shown that children who are rejected, especially neglected, by peers are likely to manifest learned helplessness in social situations (Ames, Ames & Garrison, 1977; Earn & Sobol, 1983; Goetz & Dweck, 1980; Hymel, 1983). All of these studies are based on the proposition that attributional style identifies children who show learned helplessness deficits. In particular, the internal causes of ability and effort have often been recognized as examples of attributions differing along the dimension of stability and specificity. It is believed that children, who tend to attribute failure to stable factors beyond their control such as low ability, are learned helpless. In contrast, children who tend to attribute failure to less stable modifiable factors under their control, such as low effort, are called mastery-oriented. Thus, attributions for failure are considered critical for designating children helpless vis-à-vis mastery-oriented ones.

Recently learned helplessness in children has been examined in social situations. The differing levels of social acceptance of children have been linked to their attributions, goals and behaviours. For the measurement of sociometric status of children, several methods do exist. Yet, the studies to be reviewed have adopted the method of "peer nomination". This technique requires children to nominate the three classmates whom they especially like and the three classmates whom they like the least. Children who receive a high number of positive nominations and a low number of negative nomination are called 'popular'. In contrast, children who receive high on rejection and low on acceptance are labelled 'rejected'. Children who score low on both acceptance and rejection are designated 'neglected', and children who receive high acceptance and high rejection are called 'controversial'. Finally, a fifth group consists of children who receive an intermediate number of positive and negative nominations. Children of this 'average' group do not show a distinct behavioural pattern in social situations. The other four groups indicate characteristic behavioural patterns. Hence these four groups are generally studied in relation to a variable of interest.

With a view to examining the relationship between sociometric status and helplessness, Ames, Ames and Garrison (1977) asked children to indicate attributions for hypothetical positive and negative social situations. They also classified children into categories of high status children (comprising both popular and controversial ones) and low status children (comprising both rejected and neglected ones). Ames *et al.* found that high status children make internal attributions for positive events and external attributions for negative events. On the contrary, low status children make external attributions for positive events and internal attributions for negative events.

Hymel (1983) also examined the relationship of children's causal attributions for hypothetical positive and negative social events. Status groups were derived on the basis of ratings received from classmates on a 5-point preference scale. Groups of popular children (average score greater than one standard deviation above the class mean) and unpopular children (average score lower than one standard deviation below the class mean) were compared. Attributions were collected using an open-ended interview. Children then rated their attributions on internal-external and stable-unstable causal dimensions. Popular children made more internal attributions for social success than unpopular children.

In another study, Earn and Sobol (1983) investigated causal attributions for hypothetical positive and negative social events. They employed open-ended interview with each child. Ten categories of causal attributions were found. Popular children used luck less often in explaining either success or failure outcomes and saw failure as due to the other child's motives more often than any of the other status groups. Rejected and neglected children saw success as due to the other child's assessment of self more often than popular and controversial children. Finally, neglected children saw failure as due to personality interaction more often than any of the groups. When attributions were coded in terms of the causal dimensions of internality, stability and controllability, it was found that popular children used controllable dimensions more often than the other groups.

In combination, these studies suggested that popular children are not likely to exhibit learned helpless behaviour in so far as they make attributions which are indicative of the belief that they have control over social outcomes. Second, rejected children perceive social success as less internal and stable, and thus, may be prone to helplessness. Third, neglected and rejected children are more likely to make attributions which are similar to those of children who display learned helplessness. However, these studies do not provide information regarding the behavioural consequences. It is not clarified whether attributions made by rejected and neglected groups are accompanied by the behaviours associated with learned helplessness. The study of Goetz and Dweck (1980) is the only investigation on this issue, it merits detailed consideration.

Goetz and Dweck (1980) used fourth and fifth graders who participated in three different testing sessions. In the first session, children were administered two types of sociometric testing: peer nomination and peer rating. In the second session, perception of control and causal attributions of children were measured with the help of a questionnaire. The control questions involved a measure of the children's perception of ease in averting social rejection prior to entering a social situation and the children's perceived control over social outcomes after rejection. Causal attributions were measured by presenting four hypothetical social situations in which social outcome was rejection. Children rated five different causes for the social failure: (a) personal incompetence in making and keeping friends, (b) incompatibility in that the rejecter did not like some personal trait of the child, (c) an enduring trait of the rejecter, (d) a misunderstanding, and (e) the chance mood or circumstances which momentarily affected the rejecter's decision. The attributions excepting the first were considered surmountable by the child. In the third session, a social situation was simulated. Children attempted to get admitted to a pen-friend club by producing a message for a confident pen-friend committee member. All children were first provided with rejection feedback. In order to measure goal-directed behaviour as a response to social rejection, this feedback was followed by an opportunity to send another message in order to get admittance to the pen-friend club. Goal-directed behaviour changes as response to the social failure was measured by the amount of new information in the post-rejection message.

The investigators analyzed both cognitions and behaviours of children categorized into different sociometric groups. Although the tendency to attribute social rejection to incompatibility, a trait of the rejecter, a misunderstanding, and the chance mood of the rejecter revealed no significant differences among social status groups, there were significant differences in their tendency to attribute social rejection to personal incompetence. It was shown that there was a tendency for neglected and rejected children to attribute social rejection to personal incompetence more often than controversial and popular children.

The analysis of behaviour obtained from the simulated social situation provided useful information. There were no group differences in informational units in the initial message before rejection. However, there were significant differences among the groups in the percentage of increase of informational units following rejection. It was revealed that rejected and neglected children showed less of an increase in informational units following rejection than popular, controversial and average children. Further analysis showed that neglected children indicated a lower percentage increase following rejection than rejected children.

Overall, the studies show empirical evidence for the role of peer network in the context of learned helplessness. Neglected and rejected children tend to attribute social rejection to their personal incompetence and thus demonstrate attributions which are indicative of learned helplessness. The results obtained regarding behaviours are also consistent with the attribution findings as neglected and rejected children showed as smaller change in information units than popular, controversial, and average children following initial reiection.

School Socialization

School provides an experiential world where much of achievement cognitions are shaped. The learning-teaching processes, constant evaluation and resulting feed-backs offer inputs for building one's sense of performance and achievement. Teachers' orientation interacts with existing set of cognitions moulded by parents. As a contrast to the home-specific back-ground of each child, school functions as a leveller and provides a common setting for behaviour formation. Despite such communality of school experiences, differences creep into students' cognitions in subtle ways.

The academic performance of students is a product of a complex process in which a multitude of factors interact. A significant aspect involves teachers. Teachers constitute an important dimension of educational process and they influence students' performance directly through their communication and teaching methods. However, there are more subtle ways of influencing students' learning. The expectations and covert communication of teachers may bring about certain specific outcomes.

It is possible that teachers may hold differential attitudes to different categories of students. The differential expectations of teachers with respect to boys and girls is a well-documented case. Although there are no empirical studies relating to the role of teachers' socialization in the context of students' helplessness, some investigations in the area of school socialization suggest conceptual leads. More specifically, it has been shown that teachers' socialization is associated with the development of students' mastery-oriented vis-à-vis maladaptive orientation.

As suggested earlier, sex-difference among children is worth considering. The confidence with which they approach challenging intellectual achievement situations is particularly intriguing since it emerges at an early age, when girls and boys do not seem to differ in terms of their relevant reinforcement histories. If any thing, girls should come to expect greater academic achievement, since in the primary years they receive consistently higher grades.

It has been suggested that the sex-differences in children's confidence may not be 'real' at all, and that it may reflect no more than the attempts of both the sexes to present themselves in a socially desirable light (Hill & Sarason, 1966; Sarason, Davidson, Lighthall, Waite & Ruebush, 1960). While there may be some truth to this argument, it cannot adequately account for the large body of research that demonstrates girls' lesser confidence in their intellectual abilities. Studies conducted by Lenny (1977) showed that the sex-differences outlined above appear to be quite "real".

This sex-difference is typically found with adult evaluations but does not seem to occur with peer evaluations (evaluation of the same sex). Indeed, Dweck and Bush (1976) found boys and not girls showing helplessness, when peers delivered failure feedback. Therefore, it is not children's general histories of socialization in achievement situations that have taught boys and girls a stereotyped response to failure. Rather, it appears to be their specific experiences with specific classes of evaluations that determine how they interpret and respond to feedback. Although the greater helplessness of girls is not generalized to all evaluations, the fact remains that throughout children's, academic careers the major evaluators of their work are adults. It is thus of great importance to determine precisely what aspects of adult-child interaction lead to helplessness or mastery-orientation.

Even a cursory glance at school classroom should be sufficient to convince one that girls' helplessness does not stem from teachers' negative stereotypes of them or their abilities. Research amply supports the view that girls are the ones who are favoured by teachers on almost every countenance. They are the ones who shine academically over this period. Girls consistently receive higher grades than boys (McCandless, Roberts, & Starnes, 1972), outscore boys on tests of reading achievement, receive less criticism from teachers (see Brophy & Goode, 1974), and are perceived by teachers to be the possessors of the superior intellectual and personal virtues (Coopersmith, 1967; Digman, 1963; Stevenson, Hale, Klein & Miller, 1968). Moreover, girls themselves believe that teachers consider them to be smarter and hard working and that teachers like girls better (Dweck, Goetz & Strauss, 1980). The roots of girls' helplessness must lie, then, in more subtle aspects of adult-child evaluative interactions. The pattern for boys and girls in their classes are to be analyzed.

The focus was on teachers' use of negative feed-back: its frequency relative to positive feed-back, its typical referents, the specificity of its use, and teachers' attributions that accompanied their feed-back. To examine all these, Dweck, Davidson, Nelson and Enna (1978) examined teachers-students interaction in fourth and fifth grade class rooms. The trained observers coded every instance of evaluative feed-back received from the teachers during academic subjects. The observers noted whether the feed-back referred: (a) intellectual aspects of academic work (e.g., correctness of answers, quality of ideas), (b) non-intellectual aspect of academic work (e.g., neatness), and conduct. In addition, they recorded the explicit attributions that teachers made for children's success and failures.

Boys and girls did not differ in the absolute frequency of feed-back they received for intellectual aspects of their work or in the proportion of this feed-back that was positive or negative. In other words, the two sexes were quite similar in actual success and failure feed-back for intellectual matters. However, there were striking differences in the receipt of negative feed-back for non-intellectual matters. Boys received far more criticism than girls for their conduct and for the non-intellectual aspects of their work. In fact, when examining all of the negative feed-back that boys received in the class room, nearly two-third was directed at non-intellectual matters. Even if one looks only at the feed-back that was directed towards the children's work, nearly half (45%) of the work-related criticism that boys received referred to aspects of their performance that could not reflect on their intellect. The girls, however, received relatively little criticism for non-intellectual matters. Thus, the proportion of all negative evaluations that was related to the intellectual quality of their work was extremely nearly 90 per cent. Further, while teachers only infrequently made explicit attributions for children's failures, they were eight-times more likely to attribute a boy's failure to insufficient effort than they were a girl's. The sex differences in the positive evaluations that the teachers gave were also in the predicted direction, although the results were not as striking as they were for the negative evaluations.

Thus, it appears that when boys receive a negative evaluation, their history of classroom feedback can provide many plausible and readily available interpretations. Boys can more easily than girls see a negative evaluation as a reflection of the teachers' overall attitude toward them, or they can view it as a reflection of the non-intellectual aspects of their school-work. Finally, even if boys view a negative evaluation as resulting from inadequacies in the intellectual quality of their work, the teachers' explicit attributions make it more likely that they will attribute their failure to a lack of motivation.

One may wonder at this point whether this differential treatment of boys and girls in the classroom actually causes the interpretations that boys and girls give for their successes and failures. It is important to note that the issue is whether such feedback will influence the interpretations they give to subsequent evaluations. To address this issue, Dweck *et al.* (1978) simulated the two reinforcement histories that were characteristic of what happened to girls and boys in the classroom. That is, children performed on a task which could be evaluated both in terms of the intellectual quality of their performance (i.e., correctness of the solution) as well as its non-intellectual aspects (e.g., how neatly they printed their answers); and the task was arranged so that all children would succeed on some trials and fail on others.

Children in one group (half of whom were males and half of whom were females) were given a reinforcement history similar to what boys receive in the classroom. That is, the negative feedback given by the evaluator referred sometimes to the intellectual quality of their work and sometimes to non-intellectual aspects. Children in the second group (also half male and half female) were given a reinforcement history more characteristic of what girls experience in the classroom; (i.e., the evaluator's criticisms referred exclusively to the incorrectness of the child's solution). The children then all performed on a second task on which they received failure feedback that did not have a clearly specified referent; and the children were asked to give an explanation for the negative evaluation that they received. In accord with prediction, children of both sexes who received the feed-back that boys typically receive give the attribution that is more characteristic of boys. That is, most of them attributed the negative evaluation to insufficient effort. In contrast, children of both sexes who received the feed-back girls receive in the classroom overwhelmingly attributed their negative evaluation to their abilities. Thus, this research clearly demonstrates that the differential treatment of boys and girls that Dweck *et al.* (1978) observed in the classroom can indeed have an impact on the subsequent interpretations that children make for the outcomes they experience in achievement situations.

There is an interesting irony in how girls come to develop the pattern of achievement-related beliefs that seem to hinder them when they confront intellectual challenges. The irony is that they seem to develop this maladaptive pattern as a consequence of their more favoured treatment by teachers (e.g., less criticisms: trying hard enough). While this differential treatment may reflect, in part, differential responding to boys versus girls for the same behaviours, it also appears to be the case that the behaviour of the two sexes warrants such differential treatment (Serbin, O'Leary, Kent & Tonick, 1973; Etaugh & Harlow, 1973). That is, it is likely that girls actually are better behaved and more likely to work hard in order to do well and please the teacher. In other words, it appears to be girls' greater compliance to the demands of elementary school that results in their more "favoured" treatment by teachers which, in turn, contributes to girls' failure to develop the achievement orientations that are necessary to succeed later in the really challenging areas. It is also likely that girls' greater compliance to demands of the elementary school will affect their achievement orientations in more direct ways as well. That is, when a child generally does try hard to do well and please the teachers, not only should the teacher be less inclined to attribute the child's difficulties to insufficient effort, but independent of any teacher feed-back, the child herself/himself should be less inclined to attribute his/her difficulties to insufficient effort. Unfortunately, this should result in a greater inclination to attribute one's difficulties to insufficient ability even when the most realistic and adaptive attribution in a given situation may be that a little more effort than usual and/or an alternation of strategies was needed.

In a different research tradition, the role of teachers orientation has been documented. Rosenthal and Jacobson (1968) examined the effect of teachers' expectation on students' performance. In class-room situation, they experimentally manipulated the level of teachers expectation. In the first condition, teachers were given impressions that the students were bright. In fact the students were of average standard. In another condition, teachers were not given such high expectation of students performance. Teachers in these two groups were allowed to interact with students for quite some time.

At the end of planned interventions, the abilities of students were measured to find out the changes. It was shown that students in the high expectation group registered 20-point gain in their intelligence quotients. No such gain was shown for the students in the control group. The level of intelligence is generally considered relatively stable. When an increment was shown in this stable feature, it deepened the belief that remarkable changes could emerge in other domains of skill. Rosenthal and Jacobson (1968) have described this effect as Pygmalion effect in the classroom. The effect denotes that certain positive changes are likely when high expectation is involved.

Sahoo and Tripathy (1993) investigated the role of teachers' expectation and socialization emphases. They sampled eighth and ninth graders from two sets of school in a state of India. One set of school have had commendable academic records at the Secondary Board Examination for last ten years. In contrast, the other set of schools have had consistently poor record for last ten years. It was assumed that students of the first set of schools had bright academic record as well as mastery-orientation whereas students of the second set of schools had poor academic results and learned helplessness orientation. This was assumed on the basis of the predicted relationship between achievement and mastery-orientation.

The empirical examination of academic records, helplessness test score, attributional style measures obtained from these two groups of students confirmed the basic assumptions. The students of the first group of schools revealed higher academic grades, showed less helplessness, and had less insidious attribution styles of internality, globality and stability for explaining negative events compared to students of the latter group of schools.

Sahoo and Tripathy (1993) asked teachers of these two groups of schools (i.e., teachers of MO and LH students) to indicate the expected age at which their students show a specific activity or skill. A number of social and academic skills were presented. These included activities such as "consulting teachers for their career plan," "searching for books independently" and "inviting friends of the opposite sex". The socialization questionnaire also asked teachers to indicate their attitude towards certain emphases such as negativism, autonomy, tolerance, and value of effortfulness. However, the results did not reveal significant difference across two groups of teachers except on dimensions of acceptability and negativistic attitude. Teachers of MO students showed greater degree of acceptability than did teachers of LH students. Furthermore, teachers of LH students revealed greater negativistic attitude than did teachers of MO students.

TABLE 3.1: Mean Socialization Scores of Teachers of Mastery-Oriented and Learned Helpless Students

Socialization Emphasis	*Teachers of MO Students*	*Teachers of LH Students*
Negativistic attitude	31.08	35.54
Autonomy	18.32	18.36
Acceptability	14.03	10.47
Tolerance	1.74	2.92

The greater degree of acceptability on the part of teachers of MO students relative to the teachers of LH students is consistent with theoretical expectation. These teachers of MO participants are more accepting of their students. It can be postulated that the liberal attitude of these teachers helps students in adopting broader strategies for correcting their behaviour. In other words, their sense of acceptability emphasizes a liberal approach and this approach appears instrumental in strengthening competence in students.

It is further shown that teachers of LH children show more negativistic attitudes than do teachers of MO children. Negativistic socialization implies emphasis on rigidity, inflexibility and traditionalism. It is conjectured that teachers emphasizing such school socialization restrict the development of associative bond in the students. In other words, students exposed to this kind of socialization are likely to show non-contingent beliefs. It is also possible that teachers showing negativistic orientation transmit their attitudes to their students, even if they are not aware of it. Consequently, such beliefs restrict students' exploration and prevents them from learning a wider range of skills.

On the contrary, teachers of MO students are found to be less negativistic in their orientation. Their flexibility and positive approach are likely to encourage students to explore new avenues and to form new associations among events and outcomes. Students exposed to such kinds of socialization are likely to develop mastery-orientated attitude towards problem situations.

While studies reviewed in the context of school socialization provide some clues regarding the role of teachers, the methodological complexities involved in studying school influence need to be recognized. It is likely that teachers' interactional pattern shows greater fluctuations compared with parental interactional styles. Different students may evoke different reaction potential in a teacher. From the standpoint of such complex teacher-students matrix, carefully designed control studies are needed to draw definitive conclusions regarding teachers' socialization.

Helplessness-Prone Communication

Our environment is becoming increasingly verbal and verbal communication plays an important role in shaping our beliefs, attitudes, preferences, and so on. Verbal communications flowing from parents, teachers, peers, neighbours and other important figures may have explicit or implicit persuasive message. Moreover, a repeated exposure to such verbal persuasive messages may induce a sense of helplessness if the contents emphasize uncontrollability in our environment. Although there is lack of empirical evidence to ascertain this, an exploratory study (Sahoo & Kar, 1992) investigated the selective exposure to these uncontrollability-indicating, messages flowing from peers, neighbours, leaders and mass-media.

Children were categorized into mastery-oriented and learned helpless groups on the basis of median split of helplessness scores. These two groups of children were asked to indicate the frequency with which they come across some statements flowing from their peers, neighbours, leaders and mass-media. Some of these statements were competence-inducing whereas other statements were helplessness-inducing. The results showed that MO and LH did not differ with respect to their exposure to competence-related statements made by their peers. But LH children showed significantly greater exposure to helplessness-inducing statements of their peers. Similarly, LH children more often perceived their neighbours imparting helplessness-related pronouncements than did MO children. Moreover, MO children indicated greater exposure to competence-inducing statements from leaders than LH children, whereas LH children reported greater exposure to helplessness-inducing statement of leaders than MO children. Finally the findings with respect to perception of statements flowing from mass-media were in the expected direction. MO children perceived more often than LH children the competence statements flowing from mass-media. In contrast, LH children more often than MO children indicated their perception of helplessness-generating statements of mass-media.

TABLE 3.2: Mean Scores of Children's Perception of Competence-Inducing and Helpless-Inducing Statements from Different Sources

Sources	*Competence-Inducing Statements*		*Helpless-Inducing Statements*	
	MO Children	*LH Children*	*MO Children*	*LH Children*
Peers	13.84	13.04	10.52	14.46
Neighbours	15.27	14.57	11.06	14.04
Leaders	12.08	10.40	11.50	15.82
Mass Media	11.73	9.81	12.36	15.86

Children's socialization is not restricted to family. More specifically in contemporary world, the amount of time a child spends with parents has shown continuous decline. Other extra-familial agencies such as peers, other people, political figures and mass-media are gaining importance in child's life. The study geared to investigate differential perception of MO and LH children with respect to their exposure to helplessness-inducing and competence-inducing statements of peers, neighbours, leaders and mass-media offers information regarding selective attention. However, it is difficult to conclude, on the basis of this study, that children's orientations are shaped one way or the other by these statements. It is also plausible that MO and LH children "selectively" attend to statements that fit with their existing orientation. Despite such a possibility, it is necessary that the analysis of ontogenesis of helplessness in children be extended to extra-familial spheres such as peer network, political socialization, and mass-media influences.

4

CORRELATES OF HELPLESSNESS

The construct of learned helplessness is an integrative one; it interrelates a number of concepts in a predictable pattern. The predicted pattern of its relationship with similar and dissimilar concepts not only clarifies its conceptual network but also offers possibility for its prediction as well as control. Since perception of control is a core concept underlying the phenomenon of helplessness, associations with control-related concepts such as desire for control (DC) and control-beliefs are likely predictions. At the empirical level, helplessness represents the obverse of competence. Accordingly, relation with competence related constructs such as internal locus of control and self-efficacy merits investigation. In addition, the possible predictors from among personality and self-concept dimensions are likely to contribute towards a better understanding and control of helplessness. The literature in these areas, though scanty, provides testable hypotheses and future lines of investigation.

Perception of Control

The construct of control is believed to be a core concept for the prediction of helplessness (Langer, 1983). The discussion of the theory of control within the framework of the current model of helplessness would aid to a synthesised information of human helplessness. An outcome is said to be uncontrollable when its occurrence is independent of the responses (Seligman, 1975). In other words, uncontrollability refers to non-contingency of responses and outcomes. But in a lighter vein, control refers to deliberate manipulation of materials or one's responses to get desired outcome. Burger (1989) defined control as "the perceived ability to significantly alter events" (p. 246). Moreover, like perceived control, Burger and Cooper (1979) introduced the notion of desire for control (DC). As a personality trait, it reflects the extent to which people are motivated to control life events. From this overview, *prima facie* it appears that control and helplessness are negatively related.

The discussion of the association between helplessness and control would be stronger if some of the selected empirical findings are cited along with the view-points of several researchers. Like helplessness, the prediction of motivation for control and reaction to the loss of control have been tied to numerous psychological parameters of human life. These include depression (Abramson, Seligman & Teasdale, 1978; Bibring, 1953; Burger, 1984; Seligman, 1975), academic performance (Dweck & Licht, 1980), and health (Wallston & Wallston, 1981). Moreover, it has been observed that maintaining a sense of personal control would aid to cope with stress (Glass & Singer, 1972), anxiety (Mandler, 1972; Mandler & Watson, 1966), and old age problems (Langer & Rodin, 1976; Rodin & Langer, 1977; Schulz, 1980) including many other life events. Furthermore, DC could account for significant proportions of variance in a wide variety of areas including learned helplessness (Burger & Arkin, 1980). In addition to non-contingency, the expectancy of no control would act negatively inducing helplessness. On the other side, successful exertion of control would have a positive effect leading to subsequent existence of efficiency, motivation, and reduced helplessness. It is also assumed that predictability and perceived control reduce the aversiveness of stressful events; but some research evidence was found to be inconsistent on this issue (Averill, 1973; Wortman, 1976). Other findings also showed that high scorers on the measures of DC were found to be more susceptible to learned helplessness and depression (Burger, 1984; Burger & Arkin, 1980). In spite of these contradictory viewpoints, a sizable number of studies were found to be in the expected direction. A laboratory study was conducted by Geer, Davison, and Gatchel (1970) by means of instrumental control to investigate the consequences. Subjects were given occasional shock while performing a reaction time task. One group of subjects was informed that they could bring down the induced shock from 6 seconds to 3 seconds if they respond too fast. The second group was simply told that all shocks would last for 3 seconds. The findings revealed that the first group of subjects who could control showed less eletrodermal arousal (both anticipatory and impact) in comparison to the subjects without control.

In a separate study, the controlling group rated the shock as less painful and performed better on a behavioural post-test than the non-controlling group, though there was no eletrodermal differences between the groups (Glass, Singer, Leonard, Krantz & Cummings, 1973).

Above cited studies indicated the physical consequences which seem to be more or less similar to the outcomes of helplessness. Other investigations which also involve physical or autonomic reactions include a study by Geer and Maisel (1972). In their study, subjects given control over aversive stimuli exhibited lower Galvanic Skin Response (GSR) reactivity than the subjects who did not have control. Similarly, Reim, Glass, and Singer (1971) found that subjects given perceived control over the termination of aversive noise exhibited significantly less autonomic reactivity than did the subjects for whom the noise was unpredictable.

Hence, these studies clearly indicate that the physical as well as autonomic reactions are related to control. Weiss (1970, 1971, 1972) and Adler (1971) examined the consequences of helplessness in rats. In a series of experiments, it was demonstrated that the amount of gastric ulceration and loss of weight in rats is significantly reduced when stressor (shock) is either predictable or controllable. Other similar studies conducted on human samples relating to health would be useful for the analysis. Feelings of control over important outcomes for patients of heart attack (Krantz & Schulz, 1980; Schulz, 1978) and terminal cancer (Schulz, 1976, 1978) may determine their physical well-being as well as psychological reactions to the disease. Verwoerdt and Elmore (1967) and LeShan (1961) argued that probability of survival of cancer patients is related to the amount of perceived control they feel. Moreover, feelings of personal control are important determinants of kidney patients' physical well-being and their adjustment to dialysis (Eisendrath, 1969; McKegney & Lange, 1971). In the same light, Weigel, Wertlieb, and Feldstein (1989) conducted a study to examine the relations between stress, perceived competence, and contingency. The findings suggest perceived control as a moderator of the stress-illness relation.

A study by Affleck, Tennen, Pfeiffer, Fifield (1987) on a sample of 92 patients with rheumatoid arthritis was conducted to examine interrelations among various control appraisals, illness predictability, psycho-social adjustment, mood, and illness status. From the findings, it was evident that perceiving greater personal control over one's medical care and treatment was associated with positive mood and psycho-social adjustment.

It would be relevant to quote Schwartz (1964) who concluded on the basis of clinical observations that, "the depressive person is quite able to conceive of himself as causing things in himself or in other people. However, he does not see himself as having control or choice over what he causes" (p. 696). Moreover, people choose control because control improves an aversive outcome and that enables the individual to reduce pain (Church, 1964). It was hypothesised that some of the characteristics, such as, feelings of depression and helplessness, frequently observed among institutionalized aged are attributed to loss of control (Schulz, 1976). Further, Schulz (1976) and Langer and Rodin (1976) conceived that manipulation of control may increase perceived competence. Many other researchers conceived that lack of control is most devastating when it is accompanied by broad implication of the individual's self-worth (Dweck & Reppucci, 1973; Hanusa & Schulz, 1977; Hiroto, 1974).

The concept of control is not only related to health, disease susceptibility, depression, and anxiety but to other psycho-social life events too. Control is found to have a positive association with job satisfaction (Hackman, Pearce, & Wolfe, 1978; Karasek, 1979; Weaver, 1977) and related to outcomes reflecting happiness (Karasek, 1979). Control is also associated with positive self-evaluation (Hackman *et al.*, 1978). In a similar vein, Tetrick and LaRocco (1987) conducted a study on a sample of 206 subjects comprising of physicians, dentists, and nurses from a naval hospital. The findings include understanding, prediction, and control which were directly related to perceived stress. But, only control had a significant direct link with satisfaction.

Burger (1985) presented a model to investigate the relation between individual differences in the general desire to control events, and performance in achievement-related tasks. To examine various steps, six experiments were conducted on college students. The results disclose subjects' level and pattern of expectation and achievement motivation. The subjects high in DC displayed higher level of aspiration than did the subjects low in DC. They had also higher expectancies for their performance and were able to set their expectancies in a more realistic manner compared with the subjects low in DC. Further, subjects high in DC were found to respond to a challenging task with more effort and persist longer at a difficult task in comparison to the subjects low in DC. Moreover, the subjects having higher level of DC exhibited the pattern of attribution for success and failure that suggests a high level of subsequent achievement motivation.

Taking into consideration the antecedents, concomitants, and consequences of control, it can firmly be concluded that it is one of the befitting correlates of helplessness. The cited research findings not only establish the relationship between helplessness and control but also indicate vast applicability of the construct of control in various life situations like helplessness.

The concept of control finds a more formal expression in the works of Rotter. Rotter (1966) employs the construct to indicate the perception of causality. It has also generated sufficient amount of empirical data. A brief review is considered helpful in bringing about its significance in the context of my proposed work.

Locus of Control

The locus of control appears to have relation with the construct of helplessness model. The locus of control originated from Rotter's social learning theory referring to the connection between personal characteristics and experienced outcomes (Rotter, Chance, & Phares, 1972). Like helplessness, locus of control pertains to the relationship between actions and outcomes. On the other hand, Seligman (1975) views helplessness in terms of response-outcome independence. The external locus of control may be defined as a pervasive belief that personal efforts have no impact upon the outcome. In other words, the outcome is independent of or not contingent upon the response. In converse, the internal locus of control is pertaining to the belief that outcomes are dependent upon the actions, or one's responses determine the outcome (Rotter, 1966; Rotter, Seeman, & Liverant, 1962). Hence, the helplessness model seems to be congruent with the external locus of control. An individual holding generalized expectancies of external control shows the type of behaviour that appears congruent with the individual's showing helplessness (Lefcourt, 1980). Further, Lefcourt has drawn a conclusion that locus of control is an adequate personality equivalent of the behavioural pattern of helplessness.

While analysing locus of control in the light of helplessness model, careful measures should be taken up to include different findings to overcome certain difficulties. The findings of Lefcourt (1976) indicated that individuals having internal control are less quick to draw generalization about their inabilities when compared with externals. Consequently they could be better able to accept specific instances of failure. In contrast, Phares (1976) argued that individuals face greater difficulty in assimilating negative feedback (even if they are internals). Gurin, Gurin, Lao, and Beattie (1969) suggested that individuals characterized themselves as internals are likely to be demoralized, holding the belief that they are responsible for the failure. Moreover, persons experiencing setback and failure, pertaining to internal locus of control would show depression, self-denigration, and surrender of ambitions. Several research findings give evidence that these symptoms are congruous with the symptoms and outcomes of helplessness.

In different circumstances and work settings, there are instances of produced outcomes beyond one's competence. Such persons holding a belief of external locus of control are more likely to be susceptible to the external sources, in difficulty. A pseudo-self-reliant person would show helplessness trait that resembles external control trait of persons, in face of setbacks (Lefcourt, 1980). Lefcourt argued that the construct of locus of control would be useful in predicting the manner in which persons confront challenging situations and helplessness behaviour. Further, the construction of goal-specific locus of control would ascertain profiles of perceived competence and helplessness. Strickland (1978, 1979) and Lefcourt (1979) summarized literatures focused on locus of control as a predictor of health related behaviour and stress management respectively. Health hazards, like Coronary Heart Disease (CHD) and other psychosomatic disorders, along with stress and depression, are believed to be concomitants of helplessness. Naditch, Gargan, and Michael (1975) established that there is an interaction between locus of control and the discrepancy between level of aspiration and achievement while predicting depression. Naditch (1974) also found the same variables interacting while predicting hypertension.

Control Beliefs

The attempts to further conceptualize the notion of perceived control lead some researchers to action-theoretical orientation as a heuristic framework and to develop a valid questionnaire to measure control concepts.

Perception of control is relevantly related to three sets of concepts, such as, locus of control, reformulated learned helplessness, and self-efficacy. Locus of control can be either internal or external (Rotter, 1966) and represents the locus of generalized expectancies of reinforcement. Attributional style of outcomes is the central concern of the reformulated model of helplessness (Abramson, Seligman & Teasdale, 1978; Miller & Norman, 1979). The extent to which causal explanations for perceived non-contingency between responses and outcomes vary along certain dimensions like internality, stability, and globality which explain the appearance, severity, and duration of a syndrome of deficits. The third set of concepts, the construct of self-efficacy (Bandura, 1977b), refers to the expectancy that one is capable of producing the response that leads to the desired outcome. It has predictive value for initiation and persistence of behaviour (Bandura, 1980). By influencing the choice of activities and motivational level, beliefs of personal efficacy contribute importantly to the acquisition of the knowledge structures on which skills are founded (Bandura, 1997). Beliefs of personal efficacy regulate motivation by shaping aspirations and the expected outcomes and self-assurance while managing difficult tasks.

Perception of control has predictive value in important aspects of motivational, cognitive and emotional functioning that influence action. An action-theoretical perspective of perception of control has been advanced by Skinner, Chapman and Baltes (1988) that gives more central role to actions than responses. Actions are defined as goal-directed intentional behaviours and are conceptualised as consisting of a number of sequential components. The concept of perceived control is based on the observation that naive, everyday accounts of action involve an understanding of the relations among agents, means and ends (Chapman & Skinner, 1985). These three concepts are distinguished according to the action-theoretical perspective also, that leads to three sets of beliefs. "Control beliefs" refer to beliefs about the relation between the individual or agent and a specific desired outcome without any explicit reference to the means used "Means-ends beliefs" refer to beliefs about the relation between means and ends and the individual's beliefs about the effectiveness of potential causes to produce desired outcomes "Agency beliefs" refer to beliefs about the relation between the individual or agent and certain potential causes that may lead to desired outcomes. Skinner, Chapman, and Baltes (1988) studied 155 school children and established all three beliefs to be different and to be having differential relations with cognitive performance.

Control understanding changes significantly across the life span in the same individual and in different individuals at the same stage. Different periods of life present typical competency demands for successful functioning. Control does not come innately to the new born child. Realization of personal agency comes through self-observation that outcomes flow from actions and actions are part of oneself. Early experiences of non-contingency between action and outcomes not only retard present perception of control but future controllable learning situations are also hampered (Ramey & Finkelstein, 1978). Watson (1977) has identified some factors, such as delays between actions and outcomes, imperfect linkage between actions and outcomes, multidetermination of outcomes and ambiguous environmental signalling of controllable events and uncontrollable events that can impede infant's perceptions of control. Through continuous exposure to contingent situations the infant develops a sense of self as the doer, not only the receiver. The early social experiences and parental influences that enable their children to predictably control the environment promote cognitive functioning and perception of control. Peers and school also provide motivational background to the perception of control in growing children. Bhana (1985) tried to assess Indian children's perceptions of control in the cognitive, social and physical domains of school functioning by means of the multidimensional measure of children's perceptions of control developed by Connell (1980). It was found that for each domain of activity (cognitive, social, and physical) there is a developmental difference in the children's perception of sources of control (internal, external, and unknown), internal source being more important than external and unknown sources.

Developmental Aspects

Since perception of control is not an innate, rather a developed phenomenon, its developmental analysis will help to understand this process better. Perception of control or control beliefs are a composite of contingency beliefs and competence beliefs. Contingency beliefs are beliefs about the contingency of outcomes from particular actions and competence beliefs are beliefs about the possession of such actions by the person himself. These terms are similar to means-ends beliefs and agency beliefs of Skinner (Skinner & Chapman, 1984) and response-outcome expectation and efficacy-expectation of Bandura (1997). Together both terms create control beliefs.

Control belief is a personal construct that is influenced by many environmental and personal complex factors in the course of development since birth. The first such factor is the shape and functional condition of the mother's nipple which leads the new-born to accommodate its sucking reflex and experience the first link between one's own organic behaviour and environmental factors. Watson (1966) showed that even two-month old babies learn to increase simple activities like turning their heads if the action leads to movements of mobiles and also learn to enter into regulated interaction with care givers (Bruner, 1983). Piaget (1936) had also viewed this relation between own behaviour and some effects in environment that leads to development of causal schema in the first 6-12 months of life. Such means-ends contingency between own behaviour and perceptible effects in infants leads to later learning readiness and learning speed (Finkelstein & Ramey, 1977). The causal schema develops gradually through continuous exposure to means-ends contingency situations. The one-two year old child learns to ascribe internal causes to different outcomes. The child centres its attention more on "myself", "me", and "I" than on "you" or "they".

Around 3 years of age, pride comes as indicator of success and shame as indicator of failure (Heckhausen, 1982). Children not only regard themselves as personal causes of effects but also regard themselves to be able to use the particular action to produce specific outcomes that lead to the development of a categorical self. Children categorise the causal factors in different categories that determine actions and predict future outcomes. The child then moves from strong optimism to more realism. The concept of ability in preschoolers is typically an unstructured compound of ability, effort, visible outcome, objective feedback and social feedback (Nicholls, 1978). Preschoolers tend to attribute both social and school success to effort, praise and smartness and failure to lack of smartness, lack of effort and blame. Around five years children learn to identify effort or lack of it as the cause of success and failure (Nicholls, 1978). But they do not perceive effort to be limited by personal ability, which concept is developed in middle elementary school children. They know that some tasks may be beyond their capacity to solve, however more effort they put in it. But a full understanding of the intricate relation between ability and effort is established only around 12/13 years or teenage (Kun, 1977). This stage corresponds with the formal operations period according to Piaget's theory of genetic epistemology (Nicholls, 1978). At this stage, children fully understand the compensatory relation between effort and ability and know that the person solving a problem sooner and in a better way than another person has greater ability than the other person. According to Flammer (1993), the structure of a fully functioning 'control belief' is achieved at this stage. But control belief is achieved mainly in the area of schooling, where children have considerable experience. Children move from a rote memory stage in preschool, when more effort means better achievement, to the more specialised learning stage in high schools, when ability is more necessary for achievement than effort. Thus the child develops a realistic picture of his or her control perception and belief. Another concept, luck, which is a counter-concept of control, is also developed at this stage. Young children include luck and effort similarly in ability, but through practical experiences luck decreases in importance than effort because effort is more controllable and appropriate to academic situations than luck.

Parents have an important role to play in the development of control, especially the mother, who comes in close contact with the child since its birth. Kindermann and Skinner (1989) studied mother's perceptions of children's competencies in learning developmental tasks and found that mothers' behaviour to change according to children's contingent behaviour and helping the child to develop control in everyday activities. The personal control belief of parents also leads to perception of parental control in children that helps in development of personal control in them (Schneewind, 1993).

Domains of Application

Perceived control as a behavioural phenomenon is not only applicable to academic situations, but also is linked with many other important domains of life as well. Perceived control is closely associated with sense of mastery or lack of it in important spheres of life. A study was conducted by Langer (1983) to test the proposition that the aversiveness of a high density situation that limits behavioural control could be counteracted by increasing the subject's cognitive control through the presentation of information that explains and validates arousal for the experience. She found that crowding interfered with task performance, both qualitatively and quantitatively. But information about crowding was found to have a positive effect on performance in both crowded and uncrowded situations. So cognitive control was found to be influencing perceived control. Another study was also conducted to find out whether crowding is stressful and whether it helps to arouse the person and improve performance (Langer, 1983). But no such effect was found by the author. Epstein and Karlin (1974) had found that crowding actually helps in performance of simple tasks and hinders complex task performances. When a large number of people are engaged in individual tasks in a crowded place, it leads to attentional overload because of large number of interactions. Attentional overload declines cognitive activities and performance in higher-density situations (Baum, Harpin and Vallins, 1975).

Another domain of control lies in aging process and the feeling of diminishing control in the aged people. With less of physical and mental abilities like memory, reasoning power, eye sight, hearing capacity, and muscular strength, people start viewing themselves as helpless and lacking any type of control on the environment that leads to varying amounts of depression and even death in many old people. If the aged are allowed more control over their life events, then depression is greatly alleviated. Langer and Rodin (1976) had conducted a study on old-age-home residents to assess the effects of an intervention to encourage them to make greater number of choices and to feel more control on everyday events. They concluded that the physical and mental conditions of aged patients definitely improved and did not diminish further following intervention programmes that allowed greater mobility and choice to the patients in the nursing home. In a study on aged people remaining at home, Baltes, Mayr, Borchelt, Moas, and Wilms (1993) differentiated between a basic level of competence required for basic personal care and expanded level of competence which includes leisurely and social activities of the aged. These two components are interrelated, but are found to be influenced differentially by fluid intelligence, mobility, depression, and social links at different age levels. Dependence, an antagonistic term of competence, increases in old age. When personal behaviour and beliefs become non-contingent, negative outcomes, such as cognitive deficits, motivational deficits, and emotional deficits result (Seligman, 1975).

Perception of control and control beliefs also play a major role in career choices people make during the formative periods of their life. These choices determine which abilities they wish to realise, which life style they wish to follow and which types of options they forgo in spite of possessing ability for them. Rationally, people would explore all possible options, the benefits of different options, their own abilities, and their interest in the options and then choose the option that maximizes expected utility. But people are seldom rational. Due to lower expected efficacy or control belief, people eliminate and ignore many options which may even have greater benefits and material gains for the person. Control beliefs pre-empt expectancy-valence analyses. People try to eliminate vocations or careers from their consideration, which are beyond their beliefs of self-efficacy. The more control or efficacy belief persons have, the more number of career options they have. Efficacy beliefs also contribute to the development of particular interests. So occupational development not only involves acquisition of new skills and knowledge, but also the sense of personal control through which ability and productiveness are realised.

The development of perceived control and its effect on career aspirations are affected by some social factors like the person's sex and social expectations from that sex group. Although women make up an interesting share of the work force, many of them do not choose career in scientific fields, army or many other occupations traditionally dominated by men. As a result, women's potential and their contribution to the creative and economic life of a society remain largely unrealised. Similar is the case of ethnic minorities, who also fail to develop greater personal control belief due to both discriminatory barriers and socio-economic disadvantage. To overcome the problem of restricted aspirations and occupational pursuits, the individual should consciously try to eliminate the self-limiting psychological impediments acquired through cultural practices and realise his or her own true competencies to exercise proactive control over their occupational future.

Academic Attainments

Academic competencies are among the most demanding cognitive and motivational challenge that growing children face in their life. The importance of academic competencies lies in the face that academic records in the school-life predetermine public reactions to the child and the child's future occupational picture. The growing sense of personal control and self-efficacy in children serve as a major personal force in their ultimate level of accomplishment.

Perceived academic self-efficacy or personal control is defined as personal judgements of one's capabilities to organise and execute courses of action to attain designated types of educational performances (Bandura, 1977a, 1977b; Schunk, 1989). In order to be able to use the concept of perceived control for academic predictive purpose, we should be able to measure the concept across the three dimensions of usage. The first dimension is the level of control that refers to variations across different task-performances; the second dimension is generality of control that refers to control across different academic subject matters; the third dimension is the strength of perceived control that explains the degree of certainty that one can perform a given task. All these dimensions are related to everyday academic requirements and the perception of the child about his mastery to achieve these requirements. Children with a high sense of control in academic situations usually participate more readily, work harder, and persist longer in face of difficulties than those who doubt their capabilities. Schunk (1981) had studied the effects of perceived control on persistence in work and found that modelling and didactic forms of arithmetic instruction increased student's control beliefs and persistence through cognitive and motivational mechanisms. Bandura (1993) has posited that perceived self-efficacy encompasses beliefs that effort, one's own knowledge and skills and strategies all determine performance. Berry (1987) has also found that perceived efficacy contributes to memory performance both directly and by enhancing persistence. The generalised effect of control beliefs of persistence in unsolvable tasks was studied by Zimmerman and Ringle (1981). They found that students observing optimistic models during unsolvable task situations became persistent and optimistic.

Students with high perceived control beliefs were found to be more persistent and successful in college levels (Lent, Brown & Larkin, 1984). Social comparisons strongly influence the perceived control of people, especially in educational contexts where academic performances are subject to a great deal of modelling and comparative evaluation (Bandura & Jourden, 1991). Students who observe models failing in a task are affected by this observed failure. When the model is shown to have lower capacity than the students, observed failure does not affect perceived control so much, but when the model is shown to have equal or higher capacity than the students, perceived control of the students are shown to be hampered very badly (Brown & Inouye, 1978). A review by Moulton, Brown and Lent (1991) has established the causative relation between perceived control and academic achievement.

Due to causative relation, it is also logical to conclude that such beliefs affect level of achievement as well as motivation. Schunk (1989, 1991) conducted research on children with major academic deficiencies who were engaged in self-directed learning of mathematical and language skills and found definite improvement in performance and perceived control of learning skills. Frequent and immediate performance feedback are also shown to enhance control beliefs (Schunk, 1987). Schunk and others from their investigations, have pointed out three indices of academic achievement in relation to the students' control beliefs. These are basic cognitive skills, performance in academic course work, and standardised achievement tests. Moultan, Brown and Lent (1991) analysed the relation between perceived control and academic achievement from several studies. They found that when children's perceived control is raised through modelling, feedback and mastery experiences, the raised expectation is maintained in future. This is especially true in case of low-achieving students than high-achieving students. The relationship between perceived control and academic attainment is stronger for high school and college students than nursery school students. Skinner, Wellborn and Connell (1990) have found that the best predictor of student engagement in classroom learning and achievement is a combination of control beliefs, agency beliefs and strategy beliefs. Students should believe in the controlling strategy and also believe in their possession of such strategies so that they can try to be successful.

Children's academic attainments cannot be discussed isolated from the social relations around them. The children who possess adequate perceived control are pleased with themselves, view themselves to be capable of success and are more pro-social than children with lower perceived control. Mostly antisocial personalities have a history of low perceived control in childhood leading to academic failure and problem behaviours (Jessor, Donovar, & Costa, 1991). Peers of a child have a role to play in this situation also. Students with low social and intellectual efficacy are likely to move towards peers with low social and academic pursuits. Teacher's beliefs about the control behaviour of the students and their own efficacy as teachers also influence the student's own belief about their controls. Teachers with low self-efficacy or control beliefs use negative and dependent behaviour-orientation with students for academic enhancement. Teachers who believe strongly in their instructional efficacy support development of students' intrinsic interests and academic self-directedness (Woolfolk & Hoy, 1990). Ashton and Webb (1986) have noticed that teachers' personal efficacy as a teacher predicts students' level of academic achievement over the course of the academic year, regardless of their entering ability.

Analysis of Interrelations

The terms of learned helplessness and perceived control are more or less two sides of one coin, because the obverse of one leads from another. Helplessness refers to beliefs in uncontrollability of outcomes and perceived control refers to beliefs in controllability of outcomes and one's own role in controlling the outcomes. Both concepts concern the beliefs that individuals hold regarding the relationships between actions and outcomes from different points of view. Helpless individuals fail to explore their capabilities or seek out opportunities that may lead to desired outcomes.

The reformulated model of helplessness has explicated three attributional dimensions to helplessness such as: (a) internal-external, (b) stable-unstable, (c) global-specific. The perception that events are noncontingent depends mostly on the attributions people make for the causation of events. External, stable and global causes lead to perception of external control and a sense of helplessness. Internal, unstable, and specific attributions of causes lead to perception of personal control and perseverence even in faces of failure. When the persons believe that a particular outcome is more likely to happen to themselves than to relevant others, the persons are supposed to have agency beliefs and means-ends beliefs. Because a lot of outcomes really depend on the amount of effort a person puts in for it and the amount of effort again depends on the perceived capability of persons, the phenomena of 'perceived control' and 'learned helplessness' both have great predictive value in different spheres of life such as academic, career, and coping patterns. Weiner (1985b) and Weiner and Litman-Adizen (1980) have argued that perceptions of controllability are, themselves, a product of attribution process, resulting from the degree to which individuals perceive the causes of an event as lying within their control. Emotional reactions to events and situations also depend partly on the controllability of the situations. If a negative outcome is attributed to an uncontrollable personal cause, it may lead to depression. But if the negative outcome is attributed to a controllable personal cause, like insufficient effort, it will actually lead to increased vigour and better performance. In any situation, controllability or lack of it largely determines how a person feels about his or her failure and how pervasive he or she feels the failure to be. Totally uncontrollable personal causes may lead to depression and controllable personal causes to increased effort. The reformulated hypothesis of learned helplessness has used the concept of perceived control as pivotal construct in future prediction of performance and success.

Proponents of learned helplessness and control-related beliefs have separately and independently followed their own research traditions. However, a critical analysis of these constructs suggests the urgency of examining the interrelationship empirically.

The Control, Agency and Means-ends Questionnaire (CAMQ)

The Control, Agency and Means-ends Questionnaire (CAMQ) was developed by Skinner, Chapman and Baltes in 1988. The questionnaire has been adapted in Oriya to suit local conditions (Sahoo, 1987). The CAMQ instrument assesses three categories of school performance related beliefs:

1. Control beliefs focus on the children's beliefs as to whether they can control their own school performance without specifying the means or causes. This dimension is measured by two positively and two negatively worded items.

2. Agency beliefs consist of children's judgements of the extent to which they personally have access to four prior defined performance-related means, namely, effort, ability, help from powerful others, and luck. Each means is measured by two positively and two negatively worded items.
3. Means-ends beliefs refer to children's judgements of the extent to which four a prior defined means or causal factors influence school performance. The causal factors or means are effort, ability, help from powerful others like teachers, and luck. Each cause is measured by two positive and two negative items in the instrument. Lastly, there is an unknown category of items that measures the uncertainty of children about the occurrence of good or bad outcomes. This unknown category also includes four items, two positively worded and two negatively worded.

The children would answer all items on a four-point scale ranging from never to always. The scoring of all negatively worded items are reversed while adding up. The scores for each causal factor are obtained by adding up both positive and both negative scores together and dividing them by two and again adding these composite positive and negative items and dividing it by two.

Technical reports are available that describe the scale construction in detail (Skinner *et al.*, 1988). The psychometric properties and the factorial structure of the CAMQ are described in earlier publications (Skinner *et al.*, 1988). Later on, Little (1994) and his associates analysed the concordance of a revised version of CAMQ factor structure for seven populations (East Berlin, West Berlin, Los Angeles, Moscow, Prague, Warsaw, and Tokyo) using a multiple group mean and covariance structures (MACS) framework (Little, Oettingen, Stetsenko & Baltes, 1994).

The results supported strongly the equilvalence of the factor structure across the seven populations. In addition, the factor reliabilities were all acceptable, ranging from .59 to .89 with a median of .75. From these observations it can be concluded that the CAMQ is a measurement instrument with good psychometric properties and structural equivalence across samples from diverse cultural backgrounds.

The Students Behaviour Checklist

The students behaviour checklist was developed by Fincham and Cain (1984) to examine the efficacy of teacher's report as a means of identifying helpless children. This checklist asks teachers to rate on a five-point-scale the extent to which a child engages in learned helplessness or mastery-oriented behaviours in the class-room. An example of an LH items is "wants to do easy problems rather than hard ones". An example of an MO item is "tries to finish assignments even when they are difficult". The teachers rate the frequency with which a child engages in each behaviour. There are 12 helpless items and 12 mastery-oriented items in the checklist.

A composite mastery-oriented score is computed for the entire scale with reversal of scores for LH items. The authors found coefficient alphas to vary from .90 to .94 for the entire scale. An Oriya adaptation of the checklist is available for the purpose (Sahoo, 1992). This adapted version was field-tested prior to its present use. The reliability and validity of this adapted version was found satisfactory (Sahoo, 1992).

Sahoo and Acharya (1996) used this measure of control beliefs and investigated its relationship with children's learned helplessness. In addition to the measure of children's helplessness, competence ratings for each participating student were obtained from teachers. The analysis of relationship between helplessness and other control-related measures indicated predicted pattern of association.

As expected, helplessness was negatively related to both academic achievement and teachers' rating of competence. More importantly, learned helplessness was negatively associated with children's control

TABLE 4.1: Correlation Coefficients between Helplessness and Other Relevant Dimensions

Relevant Dimensions	*Boys (N = 181)*	*Girls (N = 116)*	*All Students (N = 297)*
Academic performance	–.29**	–.30**	-.31**
Teacher rating of competence	–.22**	.13	-.19**
Control Belief	–.15*	–.19	-.13**
Agency Belief			
Effort	–.28**	–.40**	-.21**
Personal attributes (e.g., ability)	–.13	–.23*	-.12*
Powerful others	–.36**	–.35**	-.35**
Luck	.01	–.08	-.04
Means-Ends Believe			
Effort	–.10	–.14	-.06
Personal attributes (e.g., ability)	.02	–.02	-.01
Powerful others	.12	.32**	.20**
Luck	.15*	.26**	.19**
Unknown factors	.09	.14	.12*

* $p < .05$

** $p < .01$

beliefs. Children who had strong control beliefs were found to score low on the helplessness scale. Control beliefs were positively associated with agency behalf for effort and personal attribute (ability). Children who believed to have control on outcomes in achievement situations also believed that they could change the outcome through increased effort. Effort is an internal controllable viable which leads to success. So success-oriented children normally depend more on effort than on lack for personal improvement. This was reflected in this study. Interestingly, a negative relationship was shown between agency for powerful others and helplessness. It implies that with increasing helplessness, children's belief in the efficacy of powerful others (such as teachers in academic situation) also declines. Furthermore, helplessness remained unrelated to the luck. This means that neither MO nor LH children perceive luck on their side.

With respect to the importance of some means, helplessness showed different pattern of association with various means-ends beliefs. Helpless children believed in external and uncontrollable means such as luck and powerful others (for example, teachers). In other words, LH children considered that success depended on help and guidance from teachers and favourable luck, not on their own effort and personal attribute (ability). On the contrary, MO children considered effort as more profitable means to bring about desired ends. These predictions were supported by this study.

The study (Sahoo and Acharya, 1996) further showed that control beliefs and agency beliefs had positive correlations with internality, stability and globality for explaining good events and had negative associations with internality, stability and globality for explaining bad events. While attributional styles (for explaining good and bad events) indicated relationship with both control beliefs and agency beliefs in the predicted directions, these viables did not show any systematic pattern of relationship with means-ends beliefs.

Prior to drawing explanatory comments regarding the relationship between helplessness and control beliefs, another research stream merits discussion.

Self-efficacy

It would be useful to throw a light on the self-efficacy theory in view of its possible link with human helplessness. Self-efficacy involves self-appraisal that the individual holds. It includes certain impressions or ideas regarding his/her capability, efficacy or competence, and activities.

The pioneer of the *self-efficacy* theory, Bandura (1977a), maintained: "people process, weigh and integrate diverse sources of information concerning their capability, and they regulate their choice behaviour and effort expenditure accordingly" (p. 212). Further, Bandura (1977a, 1982, 1986) viewed that all behavioural and psychological changes occur through the alteration of an individual's personal mastery or efficacy.

The theory postulates two related expectancies concerning mastery or coping behaviour. The outcome expectancy involves the person's belief that a particular behaviour will lead to certain outcome. On the other hand, the self-efficacy expectancy is defined as the conviction that the individual can successfully execute the required behaviour to elicit the outcome. Here, it can be analysed in the light of response-outcome independence. As suggested by Abramson *et al.* (1978), these two types of expectancies correspond to the distinction between universal and personal helplessness. The self-efficacy expectancy can be attributed to internal or personal helplessness when the individuals perceive that they cannot execute the behaviour or response effectively to elicit expected outcome. The outcome expectancy may be related to external or universal helplessness when the person believes that successful execution of his/her behaviour will not produce the desired outcome.

Besides, other antecedents and relevant outcomes of the self-efficacy model may be discussed to find out certain relationship with helplessness. The persons having stronger perceived self-efficacy would exercise their efforts more actively in the face of aversive situations. Hence, the weaker the personal efficacy the less would be the persistence and effort leading to the helplessness syndrome. Prolonged failure in the past in different life situations would lead to inefficacy which is a counterpart of helplessness syndrome. Therefore, it can be inferred that there is a positive correlation between inefficacy and helplessness. Bandura (1987) indicated that a strong belief of personal efficacy can sustain efforts when people come across repeated negative outcomes. Moreover, stronger belief of self-efficacy would give rise to higher performance subsequently (Schunk & Gunn, 1986; Schunk & Rice, 1986). The strength of one's self-efficacy expectancy determines the amount of effort and persistence in behaviour (Bandura, 1977a).

The outcomes, people anticipate or expect, are strongly influenced by self-efficacy expectancies (Bandura, 1984). In the face of a danger or aversive situation, the individuals having positive efficacy and outcome expectancy would exercise their coping response effectively so as to avert the danger. In case of perceived danger or aversive conditions, the person would rather follow precaution or hyperdefensive strategy to reduce anxiety and to avoid danger than showing a posture of resignation or helplessness (Maddux & Rogers, 1983). The minimax hypothesis proposes the individual to minimize the maximum danger in several negative life events. The persons perceiving relatively weak correlation between behaviour and outcome are more easily persuaded by the information about their personal efficacy than the persons believing a strong relationship between behaviour and outcome (Maddux & Rogers, 1983; Maddux, Sheer & Rogers, 1982). Hence, it can be assumed that the individuals perceiving a weak relationship between behaviour and outcome may show more helplessness in comparison to the persons perceiving a strong relationship, as it involves response-outcome independence. The self-efficacy theory (Bandura, 1977a, 1977b) states that personal control endows the individuals with a high sense of self-efficacy, perceived ability, or personal effectiveness for coping with an aversive or negative life events.

The investigation of Stanley and Maddux (1986b) established that self-efficacy expectancies produce change in mood. In contrast, induced change in mood produces no variation in self-efficacy expectancy. Further, low self-efficacy expectancy creates greater degree of depressed mood. As depression is one of the symptoms and outcomes of helplessness, it can be presumed and hypothesised that people with low self-efficacy expectancy may display the helplessness syndrome. Moreover, Stanley and Maddux (1986a) concluded that self-efficacy theory has a positive relationship with health enhancement behaviour and can be utilized effectively for the health promotion and enhancement. The self-efficacy theory has the potential to be useful in psychotherapy (Goldfried, 1980).

From the above discussion, it can be concluded that, self-efficacy theory has a expanded range of applicability like helplessness. Self-efficacy would help an individual to cope effectively with aversive events in order to reduce anxiety and arousal. In contrast, self-abasement would generate stress-inducing and danger-provoking thoughts, and in turn it maintains a high level of anxiety and arousal. When persons trust and admire their personal effectiveness, having a sense of positive self-concept or self-esteem, they would overcome several problems in life, approaching to a success. The self-efficacy expectancy and outcome expectancy play a vital role for the initiation, persistence, and execution of one's behaviour in different life situations. Though all the findings are not included in this section of limited analysis, it can be hypothesised and inferred that self-efficacy is one of the important correlates of helplessness construct.

While the concepts, such as, control, attributional style, and self-efficacy help to clarify the nomological network of the construct of helplessness, the socio-cultural parameters of the helplessness are likely to provide information relating to its ontogenesis. In fact, most of the Western studies of helplessness were directed towards the investigation of manipulative factors. Those studies were not pertaining to the origin of helplessness. However, in the context of Indian social and cultural system, Sahoo and his associates (e.g., Sahoo & Nanda, 1988; Sahoo & Sia, 1988) have made attempt to identify the role of socio-cultural antecedents for the development of helplessness. This has resulted in a wealth of information.

Recently, Sahoo and Batra (1997) empirically tested the predicted pattern of relationship between helplessness and self-efficacy. The study also examined the association between self-efficacy and insidious attributions of internality, globality and stability for explaining negative events. They measured self-efficacy by using a culturally adapted version of the measure of general self-efficacy of school students. In addition, domain-specific self-efficacy of the students in relation to their academic performance was also measured.

While the negative association between helplessness and self-efficacy was not statistically significant, the results showed significant negative association between helplessness and domain-specific self-efficacy ($\underline{r} = -.25$, $p < .05$). In addition, general self-efficacy was found to be negatively related to attribution of stability for explaining bad events ($p = -.25$, $P < .05$) and domain specific self-efficacy was also negatively associated with attributions of globality for explaining bad events ($p = -.22$, $P < .05$). As pointed out earlier, attributions of stability and globality for explaining negative (bad) events are risk factors for the induction of helplessness. Thus, preliminary data on the predicted pattern of helplessness and self-efficacy are available though more fine-grained studies are needed in this arch.

More recently, Sahoo and Nanda (2000) have carried out an investigation to examine self-efficacy in the group of learned helpless and mastery-oriented children. They categorized children into MO and LH groups on the basis of median split of children's performance on children's helplessness questionnaire. Subsequently, the children were compared on their general self-efficacy as well as domain (academic) specific efficacy. The comparison showed results in the predicted direction. MO children indicate greater general self-efficacy and domain-specific efficacy than LH children.

TABLE 4.2: Mean Efficacy Scores of Mastery-Oriented and Learned Helpless Students

Dimensions	*MO Students*			*LH Students*		
	Boys	*Girls*	*All*	*Boys*	*Girls*	*All*
General self-efficacy	28.89	29.95	29.44	27.06	30.14	28.60
Domains-specific efficacy	9.82	8.06	9.24	9.22	9.13	9.18

As indicated earlier, self-efficacy denotes a personal sense of control. Since helplessness measure used by Sahoo and Nanda (2000) is based on personal helplessness, the comparison of MO and LH children is likely to bring self-efficacy difference in the direction of MO children showing greater efficacy than LH ones. However, with dimensionalization of helplessness into personal and universal helplessness, a different set of predictions are made with respect to self-efficacy.

While studies of control beliefs and self-efficacy generate testable predictions, attempts to study the relation of helplessness with personality and self-concept dimensions offer other possible lines of investigation.

Personality Dimensions

The exploration of stable predictors of helplessness has led researchers to adopt two broad routes. Some researchers have directed their efforts to examine the relation between helplessness and specific personality dimensions such as type A and type B behaviour patterns. Other investigators have adopted a more general investigation of examining association with a host of personality dimensions with a view to identifying stable and reliable predictors of helplessness. Both the streams of research are helpful.

Type A-B Behaviour Pattern

The type A-B behaviour pattern is one of the personality constructs believed to be a correlate of helplessness. The association of helplessness with Type A behaviour pattern can be hypothesised and inferred from different summarized literature and studies indicated by researchers in various life events and varied circumstances. Mainly, inferences can be made taking into account the outcomes and symptoms of both the constructs helplessness syndrome and Type A-B behaviour. Further, the concomitants of Type A behaviour would be considered in the context of the helplessness model for a better understanding of the relationship between helplessness and Type A-B personality pattern.

The proponents of type A behaviour pattern (Rosenman *et al.*, 1964) refer it to a competitive, multiphasic, and achievement-oriented personality who is having a sense of time urgency and impatience, becomes angry and aroused easily. Moreover, Glass and Carver (1980) classified the major components of Type A behaviour as competitive achievement striving, a sense of time urgency, and aggressiveness. On the other hand, relative absence of these characteristics and instances among the persons are classified as Type B personalities. But it is yet to be determined whether Type A characteristic leads to helplessness or helplessness to Type A behaviour. However, taking into account the basic ingredients of both the aspects, it may be inferred that when persons with Type A personality pattern experience more failure than success they may develop helplessness. When individuals become aggressive in their achievement strivings and have a sense of time urgency, they are likely to perceive the independence of the goal (outcome) and the action (response). This perception may lead themselves to a state of helplessness. In other words, when they find that the outcome is not contingent upon their responses or they do not get expected outcome, they may feel helpless. Besides, for a better understanding of the association of Type A personality with helplessness, their hypothesised and confirmed by-products should be examined.

The link between coronary diseases and Type A behaviour has been asserted by a sizable number of studies. Rosenman *et al.* (1975) investigated the occurrence of coronary diseases among Type A persons. They found that Type A men had more than twice the rate of heart disease as Type B men had during an 8.5 years follow-up period. Jenkins, Zyzanski and Rosenman (1976) also found that Type A personality pattern is the predictor of coronary heart attacks. Many evidences in support of the relationship between hypertension and Type A behaviour were also indicated by a number of studies. Besides, various studies indicated that concentration of more catecholamine and other chemical substances in the blood stream is found in Type A persons, which has a link with coronary diseases and other psychosomatic disorders. Wright (1988) argued that some components of Type A behaviour, such as, time urgency and anger, affect the body emotionally, cause increment of catecholamine output, liberate blood sugar, increase heart rate, and facilitate more blood-flow to the large muscles. He summarized various literature concerning physiological mechanism to indicate possible connection of Type A like functioning with pathology of the coronary arteries. He also examined certain basic ingredients of Type A personality in the light of coronary heart disease. He concluded that there is an association between Type A behaviour and CHD. Some possible ways were also suggested to cope with the problems relating to Type A behaviour. The cross-sectional study of Booth-Kewley and Friedman (1987) gives a clear picture of positive relationship between Type A behaviour and CHD. Further, the meta-analysis of Friedman and Booth-Kewley (1988) provided evidence that Type A behaviour is prone to CHD. Besides, they pointed out a relation anxiety, depression, and hostility to CHD.

The cross-sectional study by meta-analysis recently conducted by Matthews (1988) gives a clear picture of the association between Type A behaviour and CHD. She reported that there is a positive and significant relationship between Type A personality and CHD in population based studies. Besides, she pointed out that hostility, depression, and anxiety are the significant predictor of CHD incidence. However, she ruled out the efficient predictability of CHD. Further, she suggested that, Type A behaviour may be an important factor for CHD events.

These studies and the earlier discussion deepen the impression that there is an association between Type A personality pattern and helplessness. However, future research investigation would provide concrete evidence in support of this assumption.

General Personality Dimensions

Instead of proposing possible relation between personality dimensions and learned helplessness, an empirical study that employed a multitude of general personality dimensions may be considered. Sahoo and Sahoo (1991) carried out such a study. They examined the relationship between helplessness (as measured by a standardized test of adult helplessness) and each of twelve personality dimensions measures selected from the California Personality Inventory (CPI). The CPI consists of 18 personality dimensions. Yet, six of the dimensions were considered irrelevant in the context of helplessness. The twelve dimensions included for the study were dominance, capacity for status, sociability, social presence, self-acceptance, sense of well-being, responsibility, socialization, achievement via conformance, achievement via independence, intellectual efficiency, and femininity. Prior to the final use of the CPI in Indian social-cultural setting, steps were taken for its cultural adaptation and validation.

TABLE 4.3: Correlation Coefficients between Helplessness and Personality Dimensions

Personality dimensions	*Industrial setting (n = 150)*	*Non-Industrial setting (n = 150)*	*All participants (n = 300)*
Dominance	–.33**	–.17	–.25**
Capacity for states	–.03	–.07	–.02
Sociability	–.17*	–.15	–.18**
Social presence	–.18*	–.21*	–.17**
Self-acceptance	–.11	–.06	–.05
Sense of well-being	–.38**	–.27**	–.33**
Responsibility	–.24**	–.21**	–.24**
Socialization	–.50**	–.14	–.34**
Achievement-via-conformance	–.43**	–.31**	–.36**
Achievement-via-independence	–.14	–.01	–.05
Intellectual efficiency	–.25**	–.26**	–.28**
Femininity	–.07	–.05	–.33

* $p < .05$
** $p < .01$

The study used adults both from the industrial as well as non-industrial setting. Consequently pattern of relationship was examined for each setting separately and also for the total pool of participants. Results indicated that helplessness is negatively related to most of the personality dimensions. Significant negative association was shown with respect to dominance, sociability, social presence, sense of well-being, responsibility, socialization, achievement via conformance, and intellectual efficiency. It was shown that interpersonal adequacy measured by traits such as sociability and social presence had negative association with helplessness. A sizable number of studies have explained the role of interpersonal relationship in people's responses in stressful situations (Burgess & Holmstrom, 1978; Cobb & Kasl, 1977; Kelman & Lowenthal & Muller, 1966; Litman, 1962; Smits, 1974). It has been suggested that there is relationship between perceived social support (resource) and effective adjustment. People with greater interpersonal resources are capable of dealing with aversive life events. This offers some explanation for the negative relationship between helplessness and personality dimensions indicative of social adequacy.

The negative relationship of helplessness with socialization and responsibility stresses the value of past experiences with life events and successful adaptation as well as willingness to accept individual responsibility to solve life problems. Langer and Rodin (1976) in an intervention design, demonstrated positive role of control and responsibility. When they induced responsibility in the elderly people in old age homes, the people exhibited a greater sense of efficacy and less helplessness than control group subjects.

Finally the negative relationship between helplessness and achievement via conformance as well as intellectual efficacy was consistent with the notion of cognitive deficit of helplessness. Dweck and her associate have carried out a large number of studies to explicate achievement cognitions of mastery-oriented and helpless individuals.

Sahoo and Sahoo's (1991) study not only examined personality dimensions but also self-concept dimensions in relation to helplessness. The nature of correlation with self-concept dimensions deserves a close-scrutiny.

Self-Concept Dimensions

For the purpose of investigation, the Tennessee Self-Concept Scale was used. The ten dimensions used were identity, self-satisfaction, behaviour, physical-self, moral-ethical self, personal self, family self, social self, global positive self-concept, and self-criticism. In the domain of identity, the individuals describe their basic identity what they are as they perceive themselves. The score on the domain of self-satisfaction describes the level of self-acceptance—how the individuals feel about the self. The behaviour score measures the individuals' perception of their own behaviour—the way they function. The physical self-reflects the individuals' view of their bodies, their state of health, their physical appearance, skills, and sexuality. The moral-ethical self-represents the self from a moral and ethical frame of reference. The personal self denotes the individuals' sense of personal worth, their feeling of adequacy as a person, and self-evaluation of their personality apart from their bodies, and their relationship with others. The family self scales one's feelings of adequacy, worth and value as a family member, whereas the social self indicates the person's sense of adequacy and worth in his or her social interaction with other people in general. The global positive self-concept represents the individuals' overall positive self-concept or the overall level of self-esteem. The self-criticism score estimates one's openness and capacity for self criticism. As with the CPI, the Tennessee self-concept scale was adequately adapted and validated in relevant social cultural context prior to its use in the study.

The result revealed a significant positive relationship of helplessness with identity and behaviour. These two positive correlations stand isolated in the midst of other non-significant correlations. Although the two positive correlations appear bit puzzling, they need to be considered in the context of Indian socio-cultural context.

TABLE 4.4: Correlation Coefficients between Helplessness and Self-Concept Dimensions

Self-concept dimensions	*Industrial setting (n = 150)*	*Non-industrial setting (n = 150)*	*All participants (n = 300)*
Identity	.17*	.21**	.16**
Self-satisfaction	–.08	–.07	–.04
Behaviour	.18*	.20**	.15**
Physical self	.11	.11	.10
Moral-ethical self	–.02	.04	.05
Personal self	–.17*	.11	.00
Family self	.06	.06	.10
Social self	.06	.03	.09
Global positive self	.02	.09	.10
Self-criticism	.18*	–.04	.05

* $p < .05$
** $p < .01$

In Western studies, the positive association between helplessness and depression has been widely documented (Peterson & Seligman, 1984). The proposition predicts that helpless persons adopt depressive posture and consequently they experience a low self-identity and show confused behaviour. However, this relationship is more likely to prevail in Western situations where most of the people experiencing helplessness encounter personal helplessness. In contrast to such Western situations, people in India experience universal or shared helplessness. This leads to very low level of depression. Sahoo and Panda (1994) have also reported conclusion that depression and helplessness remain unrelated in Indian setting.

Although the explanation offered in culture-specific terms would explain the absence of negative association of helplessness with self-concept dimensions, the reasons for positive association with respect to identity and behaviour are difficult to explicate. It can only be conjectured that helpless people perceive a fit between their own state and their socio-cultural milieu. However, studies are needed to settle this issue.

Predictors of Helplessness

Attempts were directed to identify possible predictors of helplessness

(Sahoo & Sahoo, 1991). As indicated by the regression analysis, socialization and achievement via conformance, the two of the personality dimensions emerged to be the best predictors of helplessness. Although these two measures account for only 13 per cent of variation in helplessness, their contributions are approximately half of the total variation accounted for by several predictors delineated. The identification of achievement via conformance and socialization as predictors appear to be plausible in view of their possible linkage with past experience. The specification of social presence and dominance each contributes 3 per cent of variation. Furthermore, the sense of well-being, another predictor, emphasizes the feeling of inadequacy and unwellness as a correlate of helplessness. No other dimension from the cluster of personality and self-concept variables emerges as a good predictor.

TABLE 4.5: Results of the Stepwise Multiple Regression

Predictors	*Beta*	*p*	r^2	*Total* r^2
Achievement-via-conformance	–.17590	.0051	.06332	.06332
Socialization	–.21008	.0005	.07143	.13475
Social presence	–.18923	.0006	.03217	.16692
Family self	.16279	.0015	.01628	.18320
Dominance	–.14172	.0130	.03543	.21863
Capacity for status	.15750	.0053	.00315	.22178
Sense of well-being	–.13166	.0382	.04345	.26230

* $p < .05$

Taken together, predicted pattern of relation of helplessness with other control-related variables is shown. However, an adequate comprehension of stable predictors of helplessness requires that all the criterion variables (predictors) be analyzed within the scope of a single study. The analysis and determination of weightage system would indicate the relative contribution. While some clues have been suggested by examining the linkage with personality dimensions and control belief dimensions separately, an important objective of examining a cluster of possible variables predicting helplessness remains unfulfilled.

5

APPLICATION DOMAINS

The generality of a construct is reflected in the range and diversity of its application. Over the decades, helplessness has been extended to a wide variety of application domains such as depression (Seligman, 1975).

Depression

The widespread interest in the learned helplessness model stems, in part, from the application of the theory to account for depression in humans (see Abramson *et al.*, 1978; Seligman, 1975). According to Abramson, Garber and Seligman (1980), the model of helplessness exhibits a number of parallels to depression; striking similarities between laboratory observation of helplessness experiments and experience of depression are found. The similarities pertain to four areas: symptoms, etiology, treatment, and prevention.

The retarded initiation of responses found in learned helplessness is similar to passivity, reduced psychomotor activity and reduced social behaviour of depressives. Similarly, cognitive deficit found in learned helplessness is similar to "negative cognitive set" (Beck, 1967) in depression. Furthermore, affective deficit characterizing the helpless individuals is also found in depressives.

Symptoms

Abramson *et al.* (1980) further contend that the syndrome of depression is a complex and heterogeneous phenomenon. It is therefore difficult to specify what type of depression helplessness approximates. The subclass of depression modelled by laboratory helplessness may cut across the typical ways of clinical depression. The proponents of the parallels between helplessness and depression at the levels of symptoms, etiology, treatment and prevention emphasize that the expectation of response outcome independence is the central element in helplessness phenomenon. However, this expectation of response-outcome independence is a sufficient, but not necessary condition for depression. Other etiological factors of depression may involve physiological states, hormonal disturbances, chemical depletion, heredity and other elements. Thus, depression may be induced in the absence of expectation that outcome are independent of responding. It is also possible that more than one factor may be operative in some cases. For example, a diathesis model of depression suggests that both genetic and psychological factors (e.g., helplessness) may interact to produce depression. Accordingly there may exist a subset of depression—helplessness-depression that is caused by the expectation of responses-outcome independence and is characterized by passivity, negative cognitive set, and depressed affect.

While discussing similarities at the level of symptoms, a couple of issues need to be resolved. The case of depressed affect is one such issue. Seligman (1974, 1975) originally proposed that non-contingent positive events as well as negative events can produce helplessness and depression. Accordingly the expectation of non-contingency regardless of valence of the outcome is predicted to generate helplessness deficits including depressed affects. However, subsequent empirical testing of the proposition showed that uncontrollable positive events produced performance deficits but not depressed affect (Eisenberger, Kaplan & Singer, 1974; Griffiths, 1977). Abramson *et al.* (1980) observe "Only those cases in which the expectation of response-outcome independence is about the lack or loss of a highly desired outcome or about the occurrence of a highly aversive outcome are sufficient for the emotional component of depression. Thus, depressed affect is outcome-related" (p. 28).

The intensity of sad affect increases with the desirability of the unobtainable outcome (or with the aversiveness of the unavoidable outcome) and with the strength of the expectation of the unobtainability. In addition, Weiner (1974) posited that failures attributed to internal factors (e.g., inability) produce greater negative affect that failures attributed to external factors (e.g., task difficulty). Hence, depressed affect is more intense in personal helplessness than in universal helplessness.

The other issue that is linked with the similarity between helplessness and depression involves lowered self-esteem. It is well-recognized that depressives report lowered self-esteem. Yet, helpless individuals show a wide variation in self-esteem. However, this paradox is easily removed when the distinction between personal helplessness and universal helplessness is recognized. As indicated earlier, individuals who attribute their helplessness to internal factors (personal helplessness) are predicted to show lower self-esteem than those who attribute helplessness to external factors (universal helplessness). Ickes and Layden (1978) documented that individuals with low self-esteem attribute negative outcomes to internal factors and positive outcomes to external factors, whereas people with high self-esteem attribute negative outcomes to external factors and positive outcomes to internal factors.

Parallel to this distinction between personal helplessness and universal helplessness, some researchers (e.g., Blatt, D'Afflitti & Quinlan, 1976) have also suggested that depressives do differ with regard to self-esteem. Some depressives have low self-esteem while other depressives do not have low self-esteem. From such a perspective, the similarity between helplessness syndrome and depression does not appear contradictory.

In a general way, Sahoo and Panda (1994) examined the relationship between helplessness and depression across three quasi-experimental groups: hospitalized patients, outdoor patients, and control group individuals. Indoor patients were sampled from the orthopaedic ward of the S.C.B. Medical College, Cuttack, Orissa (India). Outdoor patients were also sampled from the same ward. Normal individuals within similar socio-economic status were sampled from the vicinity to serve as control group subjects. The subjects were individually administered the Cognitive Measure of Helplessness (CMH, Sahoo, 1985a). A measure of depression that assesses both somatic complaints as well as psychological symptoms was also used.

The results indicated that hospitalized patients exhibited greater helplessness than outdoor patients. Similarly, outdoor patients reported greater helplessness than control group subjects. Helplessness was significantly related to depression. Taylor's (1979) review of the psychological literature on the behaviour of hospitalized patients reveals that "hospitals are unpleasant places to be" (p. 158). It suggests that the forfeiture of control over tasks and outcomes results in depersonalization. Additional findings of Sahoo and Panda's (1994) study revealed that there was a positive relationship between duration of stay (or frequency of visits) and helplessness. Another relevant variable, duration of health problem, also had a positive association with helplessness in case of patients. Age, however, was independent of helplessness.

TABLE 5.1: Correlation between Helplessness and Depression

Groups	*Somatic complaints*	*Psychic depression*	*Overall depression*
Hospitalized males (n = 16)	.54*	.36	.25
Hospitalized females (n = 16)	.39	.31	.42
Outpatient males (n = 16)	.53*	.41	.22
Outpatient females (n = 16)	.25	.16	.17
Control group males (n = 16)	.12	.26	.35
Control group females (n = 16)	.50*	.44	.47

* $p < .05$.

The Study (Sahoo & Panda, 1994) depicted an association between helplessness and depression. Studies of Taylor (1979), Raps, Peterson, Jonas and Seligman's (1982) supported the present study. The study, in addition to examining indoor and outdoor patients, included an equitable group of normal individuals. This inclusion denoted variation of perception of control across groups of normal, outdoor patients and indoor patients. This is useful in speculating the role of perception of control in depressive symptoms.

The congruency between helplessness and depression is better understood at the etiological level. It has been already posited in the context of the reformulated model of learned helplessness that the tendency to explain causes of bad events in internal, stable and global factors underlies the individual difference in helplessness (Abramson *et al.* 1978). The fundamental question concerns whether or not similar explanatory styles induce depression.

Etiological Considerations

Seligman and his associates greatly explicated explanatory styles as hypothetical constructs to account for the relationship network involving helplessness. Greatly supported by a methodological framework they focused on measuring explanatory styles. Peterson and Seligman (1984) observe: "we chose not to focus on the expectation itself, even tough it is more proximate to the symptoms, because we do not believe that a valid means of measuring expectation yet exists. Also, in most cases, we chose not to focus on particular explanation because explanatory style of necessity is more reliable individual difference" (p. 350). Peterson, Semmel, VonBaeyer, Abramson, Metalsky, and Seligman (1982) developed and validated the *Attributional Style Questionnaire (ASQ)*. The scale presents 12 hypothetical items. Half are good events (e.g., you meet a friend who complements you), and half are bad events (e.g., you did a project and it was not appreciated). First, the subject is asked to write one major cause of the event. Then the subject is asked to rate the cause along the three explanatory dimensions. They are required to rate along 7-point scales corresponding to the internality, stability and globality. The internality scope ranges from 1 to 7 where '1' denotes that the event has been completely caused by the individual and '7' denotes that the event has been completely caused by other persons or outside circumstances. Similarly, stability ranges from 1 to 7 where '1' denotes that the event is purely temporary whereas '7' indicates the event to be permanent. Moreover, globality also ranges from '1' to '7' where '1' represents that the event has affected one domain of person's life and '7' indicates that the event has affected all domains of one's life. The three ratings of each cause are scored in the direction of increasing internality, stability and globality. Parenthetically it may be indicated that ratings are reversed in the case of internality while scoring. Total scores are formed separately for the bad events and the good events simply by summing the item scores and dividing it by 6. Peterson *et al.* (1982) have reported reliabilities and validities of the ASQ.

Since the important constructs of the helplessness reformulation involved explanatory style, the development and validation of the ASQ offered empirical possibilities to delineate the relation of helplessness with a host of other concepts including depression.

A large body of empirical studies evinced that depressive symptoms correlate with the use of internal, stable and global causes to explain bad events. In a cross-sectional correlational investigation, Seligman, Abramson, Semmel, and VonBaeyer (1979) administered the ASQ to college students at the University of Pennsylvania, along with a short form of Beck Depression Inventory (BDI). The BDI (Beck & Beck, 1972) is a 13-item self-report instrument that assesses the severity of common depressive symptoms. As predicted, depressive symptoms were correlated with internal, stable and global explanations for bad events. Similar results were obtained when Peterson, Bettes and Seligman (1982) employed spontaneous causal explanations and the ASQ which were also intercorrelated as congruent measures of explanatory styles.

There were quite a few other studies which produced support for the relationship between helplessness and depression. Klein, Fencil-Morse, and Seligman (1976) compared the attributions of depressed and non-depressed college students for failure on discrimination problems. It was shown that depressed students tended to attribute failure to internal factors, non-depressed students tended to attribute failure to external factors. Similarly, Rizley (1978) assessed the attribution of depressed and non-depressed college students for their success or failure on a cognitive task. Depressed students attributed failure to incompetence (internal, stable, and global) and success to ease of the task (external, specific, and stable). In contrast, non-depressed students attributed failure to task difficulty (external, specific stable) and success to their ability (internal global, stable).

Although the predicted pattern of relationship was amply demonstrated in the groups of college students, questions were raised with respect to its generalization to other settings. Navarra (1981) examined the relationship in the sample of lower class women. The ASQ and BDI were used. The results supported the prediction.

With respect to the generality of the findings, research questions were general to the case of children. As with adults, two basic instruments were needed for scaling children's depression and explanatory styles. Kovacs and Beck (1977) have had developed a Children's Depression Inventory (CDI). The CDI is 27-item questionnaire that measures the severity of emotional, motivational, cognitive, and somatic complaints of depression. Each item consists of three self-report statements graded in severity from 0 to 2. The child is asked to choose the option that corresponds to how he or she has been feeling during the preceding 2 weeks.

The *Children's Attributional Style Questionnaire* (CASQ) is a 48-item forced choice questionnaire developed by Seligman *et al.* (1984). Each item presents a hypothetical good or bad event involving the child; each event is followed by two explanations, which vary one of the explanatory dimensions while keeping the other two constant. Sixteen events pertain to each of the three dimensions, half refer to good events, and half refer to bad events. An example of an item from the CASQ is given below:

You got an 'A' on a task

A. I am smart
B. I am good in the subject the test was in

The CASQ is scored by assigning a 1 to teach internal or stable or global response, and a 0 to each external or unstable or specific explanation. Scales are formed by summing these scores across the appropriate questions for each of the three dimensions, separately for good events and for bad events. Scores for each of the scales range from

0 to 8. In addition, a composite score for all positive events and a composite score for all negative events are computed by summing scale scores across internality, stability and globality. With the use of CDI and CASQ, Peterson and Seligman (1984) found positive association between children's depression and explanatory style. The explanations of bad events with internal, stable and global causes covaried with CDI scores, as did the reverse style for good events. Since initial studies of children's depression included few severely depressed children, Raps, Peterson, Reinhard, Abramson and Seligman (1982) conducted another correlational study involving severely depressed patients. The findings were supportive.

The study broadens the empirical base of the depressive explanatory style by showing it among 9-13 years old children. It also supports the observation that childhood depression is a coherent syndrome similar to depression in adults. Later studies corroborated these observations (e.g., Fincham, Diener, & Hokoda, 1987; Nolen-Hoeksema, Girgus & Seligman, 1986). Joiner and Wagner (1995) provided a meta-analytic review of studies of children and adolescents. The review consisted of 27 studies including more than 4,000 subjects. The review showed that attributional style is clearly cross-sectionally associated with self-reported depression and with clinical depression. This appears to hold across age, gender and sample types. Clinically depressed children may possess more negative attributional styles than those with other psychiatric disorder. The reviewers also find some support for the relation of attributional style to increase in depression over time. The examination of the question of relation indicated that the association between explanatory style and depression holds. Thus, the positive relation between depression and attributional style (associated with learned helplessness) is documented.

As pointed out earlier, the crucial hypothesis posits that attributional style is associated with depression in the presence but not absence of negative life events. In other words, negative attributional style is a risk factor for depression just as smoking is a risk factor for lung's problem (Peterson & Seligman, 1984). The negative attributional style puts one at risk for later depression. If explanatory style is a risk factor for depression, it must precede the occurrence of depressive symptoms because cross-sectional studies are momentary, these investigation cannot settle the issue. Longitudinal studies were needed to answer the question. Nolen-Hoeksema, Girgus and Seligman (1996) assessed depressive symptoms, life events, and explanatory style of 168 school children in a longitudinal study. They were tested five times during the course of 1 year. Children who were both non-depressed in January and had a non-depressive explanatory style remain non-depressed in March. In contrast, children who were non-depressed but had depressive explanatory style in January became depressed in March. This, depressive explanatory style predicated later depression. Several other studies using adults provide similar conclusions (Firth & Brewin, 1982; Golin, Sweeney, & Shaeffer, 1981).

While the longitudinal studies indicate the predictive role of depressive explanatory style, they do not shed any light on bad events. According to Abramson *et al.* (1978), a depressive explanatory style *per se* is not sufficient for depression. It is only when bad events occur and are interpreted by internal, stable, and global causes that depressive symptoms are more likely to surface. In order to examine the role of bad life events, Peterson and Seligman (1984) tested undergraduate students in introductory psychology class. At time 1, participants took the ASQ and a questionnaire about their aspiration for midterm grade. Students indicated the grade that would make them happy and unhappy. At time 2, 11 days later, just prior to the midterm examination, students' level of depressed mood was assessed with the Multiple Affect Adjective Check List (MAACL, Zuckerman & Lubin, 1965), a measure of transient depressed mood. At time 3, another 15 days later, immediately following the receipt of midterm grades, students again completed the MAACL.

Students were considered to have low grade if their midterm grade was less than or equal to the grade with which they said they would be unhappy. Students were considered to have high grade if their mid-term grade was equal to or higher than the grade with which they said they would be happy. Explanatory style scores were correlated with standardized residual gain scores on the MAACL depression scale from time 2 to 3, separately for the two groups. Explanatory styles for bad events predicted increase in depressed mood for students who received low grades.

The relationship between life event and depression was further clarified by a prison experiment. It was assumed that imprisonment is a bad event for most of the individuals. Within 1 week following imprisonment at one of the four maximum security prisons in New York, Ohio and Pennsylvania, 245 adults completed the ASQ. Within 1 week before their release, which varied from 1 month to 1 year, they completed the BDI. For 28 prisoners, BDI scores from the time of initial imprisonment were available, these indicated that subjects were not at all depressed at the beginning of imprisonment. At the end of their imprisonment, prisoners scored an average of 17.7 on the BDI, placing them in the moderately to severely depressed range (Beck, 1967). More importantly, their depressive symptoms at the end of imprisonment were strongly correlated with their explanatory styles at the beginning of imprisonment. As predicted, explanations for bad events were correlated with depression symptoms.

Although experiments of nature such as prison study bring out the role of life events, the interplay of confounding variables cannot be ruled out. This necessitates laboratory studies to specify the role of explanatory styles. Alloy, Peterson, Abramson and Seligman (1984) gave subjects one of three pretreatments as described by Hiroto and Seligman (1975): a condition in which a bottom-pushing terminated an aversive loud noise, delivered through headphones (escapable), a condition in which the noise could not be terminated (inescapable), and a condition in which no noise-escapable or inescapable-was experienced (no pretreatment). Then subjects were tested on one of two tasks: a task similar to pretreatment, a solvable hand shuttle box in which successful moving the hand stopped an aversive noise, a task dissimilar to the pretreatment, a series of solvable anagrams administered in a different room by a different experimenter.

According to the helplessness model, all subjects should show deficits following inescapable noise when tested on the similar noise task. However, only subjects with a global explanatory style for bad events should show deficits following inescapable noise when tested on the dissimilar cognitive task. Alloy *et al.*'s (1984) experiment supported this prediction.

In another laboratory experiment, Pasahow (1980) manipulated the global-specific dimension. Subjects with global explanations were given instructions that told them that the concept identification task they were about to take correlated very highly with how people performed on all psychological tests. Specific subjects were given instruction that described the task as a concept formation task that had little or no correlation with other tasks used in psychological experiments.

All of the subjects were then given unsolvable concept identification problems and then tested on anagrams. Subjects induced to make global attributions for their failure performed worse on the anagrams than did subjects encouraged to give specific explanations. This suggests that the manipulation of explanation along the global-specific dimension for bad events appropriately predicts deficits when bad events are imposed on subjects.

McFerland and Ross (1982) investigated the effect of internal-external dimension of explanation. They assigned female college students to success or failure feedback conditions following a social accuracy test. They also manipulated the causal explanation for performance at this task: internal or external. Congruent with the expectation, subsequent self-esteem was lowest for subjects who experienced failure and were induced to explain it internally. So, a manipulation designed to produce internal causal explanation lowered self-esteem following a bad event, whereas a manipulation intended to produce external causal explanation did not.

With a view to cross-validate the formulation, Seligman and his associates have also used several case studies. The first two such studies analyzed transcripts of actual psychotherapy sessions with depressed patients. The other study analyzed interview originally conducted with depressed individuals. In the first study (Peterson & Seligman, 1981), each causal explanation for bad events was extracted from 300 word excerpts from transcripts. Transcripts were available from the beginning, middle, and ending of successful psychotherapy with patients suffering from depression following a loss. On the basis of content-analysis, explanations for internality, stability and globality were blindly rated by experts. For each patient, explanatory style ordered the three sessions: the most internal, stable and global explanations were offered in the beginning session, whereas the least internal, stable and global explanation were offered in the ending session.

Similar observations were made in other studies. In addition to psychotherapy interview sessions, various other materials such as written compositions, diaries, letters and similar personal notes are suggested to be natural sources of measuring explanatory styles and predicting future moods.

Taken together, studies of helplessness and depression have employed a variety of strategies. These studies have led to the conclusion that a subset of depression called helplessness depression exhibits explanatory style associated with helplessness. The explanatory style of internal, stable and global causes functions as risk factors and predict later depression. However, the exact role of causal explanations of good events is not delineated in the context of depression. Furthermore, the origin of explanatory style remains unclarified.

Treatment and Prevention

Although the origin of explanatory style is not specified, vulnerability of people with depressive attributional style is clearly recognized. Seligman and his associates suggest that people who differ in attribution systematically vary with their response to uncontrollability. Over-generalization and arbitrary inferences found in depressives (Beck, 1967) seem to stem from global and stable explanation of causes. Accordingly Seligman and his colleagues suggest treatment programme based on these observations. Therapy needs to be geared to change the estimated probability of the outcome. This can be done by changing the environment in such a way as to reduce the likelihood of aversive events and increasing the likelihood of desirable events. Second, it is useful to make highly preferred outcome less preferred by reducing the aversiveness of unavoidable outcome or the desirability of unobtainable outcome. Third, treatment needs to be directed towards changing expectation of uncontrollability to controllability. If the person does not possess skill, skill-training is necessary. If the person does possess skill, awareness has to be strengthened. Finally, changing attribution from unrealistic to realistic ones is crucial. Reattribution training would aim at changing internal, stable and global explanation of causes for bad events to external, unstable and specific explanation of causes. This reattribution training is not only useful at the time of treatment programme, it is effective as a preventive strategy.

Academic Achievement

The motivational significance of the construct of helplessness emphasizes its implication for various performance domains. However, the consideration of academic performance constitutes an important element in our community enterprise. It is not surprising that a bulk of studies relating to helplessness and performance decrement have been directed to academic settings.

The Achievement Cognitions

A large body of recent literature has examined children's beliefs about their performance in intellectual achievement situations. A number of studies have examined how children view the causes of the difficulties they experience in achievement situation (i.e., causal attribution for failures); and it has been found that children's causal attributions are among the best predictors of how they will actually perform in the face of failure. When confronted with difficulty, children who attribute their failures variable on controllable factors (in particular, insufficient effort) are more likely than other children to maintain high expectancies for future success (Diener & Dweck, 1980; McMahan, 1973; Nicholls, 1975; Weiner, Frieze, Kukla, Reed, Rest & Rosenbaum, 1971; Weiner, Nierenberg & Goldstein, 1976). They are more likely to respond with an escalation of effort and, consequently, they may actually be prompted to show higher levels of problem solving as a result of confronting failure (Diener & Dweck, 1978, 1980; Dweck, 1975; Dweck & Reppucci, 1973; Weiner *et al.*, 1971; Licht & Dweck, 1984). In contrast, children who attribute their failures to factors that are stable and beyond their control (particularly insufficient ability) tend, in the face of difficulty, to lower their expectations for future successes, and they are less likely than other children to increase their efforts in order to meet such challenges. In fact, they may respond with a deterioration of effort and performance that is so marked that they are unable to solve virtually the same problems they had solved with ease prior to confronting difficulty. These children known as "learned helpless" imply that the termination of failure is beyond their control. These children are not actually facing an uncontrollable failure, but they appear to believe that.

Several investigators have tried to alter the way that helpless children respond to failure by altering these children's causal attribution for failure. That is, they have directly taught children to attribute their failures to insufficient effort in order to determine whether the children would then maintain or even increase their efforts when confronted with difficulty. The success of these procedures (Andrews & Debus, 1978; Chapin & Dyck, 1976; Dweck, 1975; Fowler & Peterson, 1981; Schunk, 1982) is important not only because of its clinical educational implications, but also because it demonstrates that children's belief about their achievements are more than past predictors or reflections—they can actually be among the causes.

When one considers the logical implications of children's causal attributions, it becomes clear why they have the effects that they do. Since one's abilities are generally viewed as relatively stable, the belief that one's difficulties are caused by insufficient ability implies that failure may well continue despite one's efforts (Weiner, 1972; Weiner *et al.*, 1971). Thus, a lowering of expectancies and effort should follow. A lessening of one's efforts should, in turn, further lessen one's chances of success. Thus, the child's beliefs about his/her abilities are likely to be confirmed regardless of the validity of these beliefs. In contrast, attributing a failure to insufficient effort implies that an escalation of one's effort or alteration of one's strategy should result in a successful outcome. Thus, it is not surprising that these children maintain high expectancies of future success even in the face of difficulty. Furthermore, an escalation of effort should be the logical consequence of such an attribution. Since, in many situations, increase in effort will indeed pay off with improved task performance (even if one's abilities are not particularly high), this attribution is likely to be reinforced. Thus, children's attributions not only have implications for the behaviour that follows failure, but the consequences of these attributions make them self-perpetuating, regardless of how accurate or inaccurate these beliefs may actually be.

A similar logic is applicable to the attributions that children make for their successes. Children (helpless) who attribute their success to variable factors such as luck should not maintain stable, high expectancies, even if they have experienced considerable success in the past. Since, one's luck can change at any minute, so too can one's success if they are due primarily to luck. In contrast, children (mastery-oriented) who view success as an indication that they possess the necessary abilities should, after experiencing success, possess high expectancies of future success on this and similar tasks. Indeed, attributions of success to ability are associated with high levels of confidence following success, while success attributions to luck are not (Diener & Dweck, 1980; Nicholls, 1975).

Thus, the helpless and mastery-oriented children differ; the distinction is marked by the constellation of achievement cognitions they entertain. When they encounter difficulties and when failures occur, the cognitions of the helpless child reflect their tendency to dwell on the present, to dwell on the negative, and to seek an escape from the situation. The cognitions of the mastery-oriented children reflect their tendency to look towards the future, to emphasize the positive, and to invest their energies in actively pursuing solution-relevant strategies (Dweck & Licht, 1980).

Sex-Difference

One of the most intriguing findings of the studies on children's beliefs about their performance in intellectual achievement situations is that girls, relative to boys, have less confidence in their ability to succeed on challenging intellectual tasks. Girls' lower level of confidence is of great interest not only because it seems unrealistic, but because it appears to have a detrimental effect in the long run on girls' intellectual accomplishments. The studies on nature of sex differences in these beliefs collect many interesting findings.

Girls are more likely than boys to attribute their failures to ability. While boys are more likely to view their difficulties on failures as stemming from insufficient effort (Dweck & Bush, 1976; Nicholls, 1975), boys are also more likely than girls to blame the valuator for their difficulties (Dweck & Bush, 1976). While this attribution may result in lower expectations and efforts in the current situations, it still allows, a boy to maintain confidence in his intellectual abilities. Thus, when the evaluation is no longer present, the child should respond with renewed hope of success (Dweck, Goetz & Strauss, 1980).

While girls are more likely than boys to use ability as an explanation for failure, they are less likely than boys to use ability as an explanation for their success. They show instead a stronger tendency than do boys to view their success as due to factors, such as luck, which imply some uncertainty about their ability to succeed in the future (Nicholls, 1975; Licht & Shapiro, 1982).

Consistent sex-difference also emerges when investigators ask children to indicate how well they expect to do on novel achievement tasks that the children are about to undertake. In this setting, girls tend to underestimate their chances for success. In contrast, the expectancies of boys are inclined to be over-estimates (Montanelli & Hill, 1969). This sex-difference can also be found when children are asked to predict future academic performances (Dweck *et al.*, 1980) despite girls' history of superior grades during elementary school.

Not only do girls hold lower expectations for themselves when they enter a new situation, but girls' expectancies are also more likely to deteriorate when encountering difficulty or heightened evaluative pressure (Dweck, Goetz & Strauss, 1980; Dweck & Gilliard, 1975); and girls' expectations are less likely to recover again even when the situation changes substantially. Dweck *et al.* (1980) found that after encountering failure, a change in the evaluation resulted in a greater recovery of expectancies for boys than for girls, and a change in both the task and the evaluator resulted in a return in boys' expectancies to their pre-failure levels. Girls, however, failed to show such a complete recovery. As the authors suggested, it may be that when girls blame their ability for their failure, the ability that they condemn is not specific to any one task. Rather they may be blaming a more general ability which would lead them to view failure on a particular task as an indication that they will encounter difficulties across a variety of achievement situations.

In the light of these sex-difference in the generalization of failure effects, it is not surprising to find sex-differences in the tasks children seek and in how they actually respond to the challenges they confront in intellectual achievement situations. Boys are more likely than girls to choose difficult tasks over easy ones both in the laboratory and in a naturalistic free-play setting (Butterfield, 1965); and once they choose to begin a difficult task, they are more likely than girls to persist until it is successfully completed. Girls, in contrast, are more likely to avoid those situations that hold the threat of failure. Furthermore, in situations where children do not have the option of choosing the tasks they wish to work on, boys are more likely to meet difficult tasks and evaluative pressure with an escalation of effort, while girls sometimes show lower achievement effort in difficult evaluative situations than in situations where success is more assured (Dweck & Bush, 1976; Dweck & Gilliard, 1975).

The analysis of proficiency in specific academic areas provides clues regarding achievement-related cognitions. Mathematics and verbal proficiency are two such areas where group differences are marked.

Specific Area of Proficiency

Mathematics (beginning in the late elementary school years) appears to be an area where, regardless of one's aptitude, one is likely to confront novel and challenging material quite often. This seems less likely to be the case in verbal areas. Once the basic verbal skills (reading, writing, spelling, vocabulary) have been acquired, increments in difficulty tend to be gradual. When a child is confronted with reading, defining, or spelling a new word, he/she can usually succeed by carefully applying the same rules and skills that are needed in the past. Thus, in most cases, children are not likely to be confronted in verbal areas with a large set of new tasks that require them to grapple with completely novel concepts.

In maths, however, new units often begin with a totally new set of concepts to be mastered, and this may require the child to think in very novel ways, ways that he/she has not confronted in earlier units or in other aspects of his/her life (e.g., conceptualizing an imaginary number or solving simultaneous equations in algebra). A careful application of old skills and modes of thinking, though perhaps necessary, will not be sufficient. Thus, to enjoy an area like maths and perform upto one's abilities, one must be able to maintain one's confidence and concentration in the face of novelty and in the face of failure, since it is a rare individual who can grasp such new concepts without experiencing a fair degree of confusion.

As indicated earlier, the achievement cognitions of the mastery-oriented and the helpless children differ strikingly. The LH children tend to enter novel intellectual achievement situations with lower expectations of success; when success is achieved, they are less likely than MO children to interpret it as a reflection of their ability (lack of confidence). When LH children also confront difficulty in intellectual achievement situation they are less likely to interpret it as an indication of insufficient effort and consequently, they are more likely than MO children to show disruptions of effort and performance following failure. This type of achievement orientation of LH children is poorly matched to the acquisition demands of the mathematics. In contrast, this characteristic of maths may serve to make it attractive to MO children who view a novel task with moderate risk of failure as challenging.

Thus, while helpless children would be expected to perform upto their abilities in verbal areas, their achievement orientations may be less well-matched to the acquisition demands of mathematics. Mastery-oriented children, on the other hand, who often show enhanced performance in the face of difficulty, might be expected to perform their best when confronting the challenges of mathematics.

When one considers this analysis along with the finding that girls are more likely than boys to be helpless and boys are more likely to be mastery-oriented (Butterfield, 1965; Dweck & Reppucci, 1973; Nicholls, 1975; Veroff, 1969), one potential explanation emerges for why males often perform better than females in mathematical problem-solving (Fennema & Sherman, 1977; Hilton & Berglund, 1974; Donlon, Ekstrom, & Lockheed, 1976; Wilson, 1972) whereas girls outscore boys on tests of verbal achievement (Anastasi, 1958; Maccoby & Jacklin, 1974; Donlon *et al.*, 1976).

The Culture-Specific and Cross-Cultural Support

An elaborate discussion on achievement cognitions and their possible relationship with helplessness and attributions raises the issue of empirical support. Although a number of studies in the Western contexts have shown children's attributions as the predictors of their later academic success/failure (i.e., Fincham, Hokoda & Sanders, in press; Nolen-Hoeksema, Girgus, & Seligman, 1986), testing of this proposition in different cultural contexts is required. While discussing the relevance of attributional model of learned helplessness, Singhal and Kanungo (1994a) have argued that the operationalization and application of the construct in educational scenarios are needed in both cross-cultural as well as culture-specific contexts.

Kanungo (personal communication) developed a scale of helplessness based on the measure of expectancies. Apart from measuring personal and universal helplessness of students, it scales students' non-contingency, emotional and motivational deficits. Although Kanungo developed it in the context of Canadian university students, it was adapted to Indian socio-cultural setting. Sahoo and Rath (1989) applied it to high school as well as college students. The predicted pattern of relationship amongst five components measured indicated the expected network of relationship. Personal helplessness was positively related to non-contingency as well as to motivational and emotional deficits. Although universal helplessness was shown to have similar pattern of relationship with non-contingency, motivational deficits and emotional deficits, the degree of association was weaker. This was in congruence with expectation. However, contrary to the conceptualization of personal helplessness and universal helplessness as two orthogonal (independent) dimensions, they were found to be strongly interrelated.

TABLE 5.2: Intercorrelations amongst Variables involved in Helplessness Measure

Sample		*Variables*				
		1	*2*	*3*	*4*	*5*
Boys (n = 57)	1. Personal helplessness		.42**	.37**	.18	.37**
	2. Universal helplessness			.14	.0	.25*
	3. Non-contingency				-.02	.18
	4. Emotional deficit					.34**
	5. Motivational deficit					
Girls (n = 43)	1. Personal helplessness		.47**	.28	.17	.13
	2. Universal helplessness			.05	.25	-.12
	3. Non-contingency				.19	.31*
	4. Emotional deficit					-.63**
	5. Motivational deficit					
All Students (n = 100)	1. Personal helplessness		.43**	.17.	-.17	.23
	2. Universal helplessness			.07	.17	.20
	3. Non-contingency				.14	.20
	4. Emotional deficit					.51**
	5. Motivational deficit					

* $p < .05$
** $p < .01$

This finding seems to be a culture-specific phenomenon. It is likely that people develop helplessness as a result of their observation of others' helplessness. In other words, the kind of helplessness experienced by Indians is mostly *shared* or universal helplessness. This conjecture explains, at least in part, the weak association between helplessness and depression, in contradistinction to the Western finding of strong relationship between helplessness and depression.

The transcultural features of the construct was demonstrated by subsequent use of Kanungo's helplessness scale in cross-cultural contexts (Singhal & Kanungo, 1994, 1996). In their first study, data were obtained from 120 Canadian and 190 Indian students with respect to their personal helplessness, universal helplessness, non-contingency, emotional deficit, and motivational deficits. Results showed that two cultural samples had lowered helplessness much below the theoretical helplessness. The groups did not differ in levels of helplessness, but a higher amount of variance was accounted by the personal and situational correlates in the case of Canadian sample than the Indian sample.

In the second study (Singhal & Kanungo, 1996), the generality of the predictions derived from the helplessness model was examined across two national samples. Data collected from Canadian and Indian university students supported the predicted pattern of relationship. As in Sahoo and Rath's (1989) study, personal helplessness was significantly related to universal helplessness; each of the types of helplessness was further related to non-contingency, emotional deficit, and motivational deficit. These empirical investigations (Sahoo & Rath, 1989; Singhal & Kanungo, 1994) not only confirmed the robustness of the cognitive measure of helplessness, the works evinced the necessity of examining the hypothesized relationship of helplessness with other pertinent dimensions such as academic attainment.

The direct examination of academic achievement is reported by two studies in India (Sahoo & Tripathy, 1993; Sahoo & Acharya, 1996). Both of these studies employed Children's Helplessness Questionnaire described earlier. Authentic academic records available from the school authorities were used. As predicted, MO children indicated higher academic achievement.

It is important to recognize that the mechanisms that mediate the relationship between helplessness and academic achievement involves explanatory style. Hence, the empirical examination of the association between explanatory style and academic achievement is very informative. Sahoo and Tripathy (1993) and Sahoo and Acharya (1996) attempted to do this. Attributional styles of children were measured by the Children's Attributional Style Questionnaire (CASQ) adapted by Sahoo.

TABLE 5.3: Mean Academic Achievement of Helpless and Mastery-Oriented Students

Study	*Orientation*	*Boys (n = 156)*	*Girls (n = 123)*	*Combined*
Study 1	MO	336.11	228.60	282.35
(n = 279)	LH	185.24	176.21	180.72
(Sahoo & Tripathy, 1993)	All	260.67	202.40	—
			(n = 181)	*(n = 116)*
Study 2	MO	38.45	44.31	40.85
(n = 297)	LH	30.07	35.42	32.04
(Sahoo & Tripathy, 1996)	All	34.33	40.33	—

Note: The maximum marks for the measurement of academic attainments were different across the two studies considered.

TABLE 5.4: Correlations between Academic Achievement and Helplessness-Linked Dimensions

Nature of Events	*Dimensions*	*Correlations*	
		Study 1 (n = 279) (Sahoo & Tripathy)	*Study 2 (n = 297) (Sahoo & Acharya)*
Negative events	Helplessness	–.32**	–.31**
	Internality	–.16**	–.17*
	Stability	–.23**	–.18*
	Globality	–.14**	–.20*
	Composite attribution	–.31**	–.27**
Positive events	Internality	–.15*	.14
	Stability	.22**	.11
	Globality	–.06	.20**
	Composite attribution	.17*	.18*

* $p < .05$
** $p < .01$

The findings of both studies are supportive, although the former support is somewhat stronger than the latter. The finding that internal attribution is negatively related to academic achievement is explainable in terms of conceptual studies of attribution variables. As pointed out earlier, persons employing internal attributions for bad events (failure) experience a sense of a lack of confidence. According to Dweck (1986), such persons emphasize *performance goals* than the *learning goals*. The emphasis on performance goals stresses the ultimate outcome (success or failure); as a result, disruptive behaviour ensues when failures are encountered. On the contrary, learning goals emphasized by mastery-oriented person consider possibilities at the level of strategies; hence inappropriate strategies are substituted by appropriate strategies when failures are encountered. Thus, maladaptive (LH) orientation retards academic performance whereas adaptive (MO) orientation facilitates performance.

Similarly persons adopting stable attributions for negative events view bad events (failure) to be permanent for a longer period of time. This maladaptive style may not prompt them to change their strategies periodically. Hence, a streak of failures continues over a period of time. Globality is also predictive of academic performance. Global explanation of cause for bad events is found to be detrimental to academic attainment. Globality for explaining bad events brings problem into area of success and failure. The individual might have experienced failure in some areas of his or her life. It is likely that such individuals transfer their failure cognition to other areas of life. For instance, a child experiencing failure in establishing adequate interpersonal relationship may transfer such feelings of uncontrollability to the area of academic performance.

While internal, stable and global explanations for bad events have been found to be maladaptive to academic achievement (success), these dimensions used for explaining good events are found to be adaptive to achievement.

The examination of sex difference indicates that girls report greater helplessness than boys in Sahoo and Tripathy's (1993) study whereas boys indicate greater helplessness than girls in Sahoo and Acharya's (1996) study. However, within each sex group, the patterns of relationship between attributions and achievements hold. The sex difference in helplessness may be due to rural urban difference in plural India. Girls in rural areas of India encounter more negative events than do girls in urban sector.

Implications

The observation that explanatory styles associated with children's helplessness vis-à-vis mastery-orientation have predictive value for future academic attainment has both theoretical as well as practical implications.

First of all, attributions are not only good predictors of academic achievement, the attributions are also stable over a period of time (Fincham, in press). Fincham also demonstrates general pattern of children's responding revealed by their attributions. The attributional pattern children demonstrate in laboratory tasks generalize to other tasks as well (Rholer, Blackwell, Jordan & Walters, 1980). There is also consistency in child's response to failure in different life situations (social, academic, and sports). Furthermore, the distinct LH or MO response pattern is manifest in naturalistic settings.

Based on these observations, a number of studies have investigated interventions designed to remediate LH behaviour (Forstering, 1985). A common assumption is that learned helplessness is maladaptive and internal, stable and global explanatory styles for bad events produce performance deficits. However, there are quite a few subtle issues that merit close scrutiny. Fincham (in press) points out a number of such relevant issues.

First, there is evidence to show that LH children have greater difficulty mastering new materials when it is preceded by a confusing task than when it is not preceded by a confusing task (Licht & Dweck, 1984). It implies the interaction between response pattern and task material. For example, ordering task materials from easy to difficult may help LH children; it may disadvantage MO children whose learning is facilitated by challenging nature of the task.

Second, LH response has been related to the pattern of evaluative feedback in the classroom rather than the absolute amount of positive and negative feedback. The LH response pattern is related to the proportion of negative feedback given for intellectual (e.g., accuracy) versus non-intellectual aspects of performance (Dweck *et al.*, 1978). It suggests that teacher, while dealing with LH children, must not limit negative feedback to academic performance but need to include feedback pertaining to non-intellectual domains.

Finally, it is also a legitimate topic to study whether or not LH response has coping functions. Although attribution of lack of effort for failure is considered adaptive and attribution of low ability for failure is viewed maladaptive, are there no tasks that appropriately require ability? This question needs to be probed. While bulk of the intervention studies have been geared to change from ability attribution to effort attribution (Dweck & Reppucci, 1973), future research is needed to make definitive conclusion regarding the dysfunctional nature of ability attribution in all circumstances.

Work Inefficiency

The conceptual advances in the area of achievement motivation are likely to be applicable to work behaviour. Work settings present work goals and employees are expected to successfully accomplish work objectives. The generality of LH and MO responses needs to be examined in the context of organizational behaviour. However, there are no Western studies to shed light.

A fundamental proposition that has remained uninvestigated concerns the role of helplessness in job inefficiency, particularly in the context of the Indian socio-cultural system. Although a number of researchers have suggested that Indian socialization influences affect work, few systematic investigations exist to document the relationship. Kanungo and Misra (1985) in their analysis of declining work motivation in India have indicated that socialization in India produces three types of behavioural dispositions that are relevant in the context of work motivation. One such disposition is personal helplessness. Since there is a great deal of carry-over effect from family norms to work norms in India. Personal helplessness as an end-product of past socialization is likely to affect work motivation.

A distinction, however, must be made between personal helplessness and universal helplessness. Western studies have shown an individual's perception that he/she is helpless may be orthogonal to his/her perception that others too are helpless. These two dimensions (personal and universal helplessness) categorize individuals into four clusters: (a) high on personal helplessness and high on universal helplessness; (b) high on personal helplessness and low on universal helplessness; (c) low on personal helplessness and high on universal helplessness, and (d) low on personal helplessness and low on universal helplessness. It is important to recognize that people high on personal helplessness and low on universal helplessness are really helpless. They demonstrate a passive attitude towards environment. They believe that the external environment controls them, rather than that they control the environment. Thus, their attitude is likely to make them indifferent to work demands and work satisfaction.

People low on personal helplessness and high on universal helplessness are said to have a mastery-orientation towards the environment. They believe they can control the environment even if others have failed. This attitude brings them closer to work and organizations and this will produce certain work-related outcomes. Thus, it is predicted that personal helplessness undermines the belief that certain job behaviours will produce certain outcomes. Personal helplessness is also associated with motivational deficits, whereas it is negatively related to satisfaction. Universal helplessness, on the contrary, is likely to have a weak relationship with these dimensions of non-contingency, motivational deficits and satisfaction.

Sahoo (1991) undertook a study to test these predictions and to provide inputs for helplessness remediation programmes. The participants in this study were sampled from educational, financial, and medium scale industrial organizations of Eastern India. There were 220 adult (170 males and 50 females) participants. Their ages ranged from 30 to 55 with an average age of 36.5 years. Most of the participants had bachelor's degrees while college teachers had masters' degree in their respective subjects. In each organization, employees of two different job levels were sampled.

Employee's Helplessness Questionnaire

The Employees' Helplessness Questionnaire (EHQ) is a multi part questionnaire developed by Kanungo and Sahoo (1988) to measure employee helplessness (both personal and universal), non-contingency, emotional, and motivational deficits.

The part measuring personal helplessness is formed like a Likert-type scale. There are twelve items in this part. Each item gives information about a participant's personal helplessness. For instance, there are sentences like "As an employee, I feel totally in control/totally helpless". The sentence is indicative of the individual's feeling about himself/herself. A six-point scale is appended to each sentence, indicating various degrees of helplessness, with '0' and '5' as the two extremes indicating full confidence (0) and total helplessness (5) experienced by the individual in handling different problems in his/her work situations. The figures, 1, 2, 3 and 4 are indicative of an increasing feeling of helplessness shown by the individual, in between these two extremes.

Similarly, the part measuring universal helplessness is also formed like a Likert-type scale. There are twelve items in this part also. Each item gives information about a participant's sense of universal helplessness. For instance, there are sentences like "people are totally in control/totally helpless". The sentence helps to reveal the participant's feeling regarding the extent of helplessness of his/her co-workers, in similar work situations. Responses to these items indicate the extent of a participant's sense of universal helplessness. As with the personal helplessness measure, a six-point scale is given for each item.

The part measuring non-contingency includes eleven items. Each item indicates the subject's belief that behaviour and outcomes are independent of one another. At the side of each item, four alternatives are indicated: strongly approve, approve, disapprove, and strongly disapprove. The subject chooses one of the response categories to report his/her reaction to each item. For example, there are sentences like "No matter how much I try, I doubt, I would be able to live up to any of my organization's expectations". Approving this item strongly indicates the presence of greater non-contingent belief.

The part measuring emotional deficit includes seven items. Each item indicates the degree of lack of work satisfaction that an employee reports. The response categories provide four alternatives, as given for non-contingent items. For example, there are sentences like "I am quite happy and satisfied with life in my organization". Participants who approve the statement are satisfied with the organization and those who disapprove are dissatisfied with the organization.

The part measuring motivational deficits includes four items. There are sentences like "When I feel that I did not get the promotion, I deserved, I fight for it". The response alternatives provided are similar to those for non-contingency and satisfaction. Persons strongly disapproving the items show a high degree of motivational deficit.

Part 3 of the questionnaire seeks personal information concerning the participant's age, sex, income level, experience, work hours, social activities and the like.

The psychometric characteristics of this scale have been reported elsewhere (Sahoo & Tripathy, 1990). The internal consistency of the personal and universal measure is very high. A Cronbach coefficient α (alpha) value of .85 and .83 were obtained for the personal and universal helplessness scales respectively. Similarly, Cronbach's alpha of the non-contingency part was .79, .81 and .74 were for the emotional and motivational deficit scales. In sum, measures of high internal consistency offer satisfactory evidence for subsequent use in research.

However, the previous study (Sahoo & Tripathy, 1990) has indicated the possibility of carry-over effects from the personal helplessness measure to the universal helplessness measure. With a view to getting around this problem, measures were administered in two different sessions separated by a gap of at least two weeks. The measures of personal helplessness and universal helplessness were not administered in the same session.

The participants were individually contacted at their work place, measures were administered to each one of them individually. The participant was asked to respond to each item according to instructions indicated on the test booklet. It was clearly indicated to the participants that there were no correct or incorrect answers. Care was also taken to assure them that their responses would remain confidential and would be used only for research.

During the first session, the measures of personal helplessness, non-contingency, satisfaction, motivational deficits and personal data were administered. The measure of universal helplessness was given in the second session; a gap of at least two weeks separated the sessions. Responses were scored with the help of scoring keys and were statistically analyzed.

The analysis was first geared to examine some of the psychometric properties of the Employees Helplessness Questionnaire (EHQ). Cronbach's alpha computed for each dimension showed higher internal consistency for each sub-scale. The indices ranged from .74 to .85. In addition to the previous study (Sahoo & Tripathy, 1990), this study provided further evidence on the efficacy of this relatively new measure. Moreover, the EHQ readministered to 100 employees of the original pool after a gap of three months yielded reliability data. The test-retest reliability, as shown in Table 5.5, was found to be quite satisfactory. Apart from its test-efficacy, a number of predictions were also empirically tested.

TABLE 5.5: Intercorrelations of Helplessness Dimensions

Variables	*Alpha* ($n = 220$)	*Retest* ($n = 100$)	*Dimensions*			
			1	*2*	*3*	*4*
1. Personal helplessness	.85***	.67***	—			
2. Universal helplessness	.83***	.71***	.42**			
3. Non-contingency	.79***	.61***	.37**	.13*	—	
4. Emotional deficit	.81***	.64***	.39**	.09	.21**	—
5. Motivational deficits	.74***	.59***	.25**	.04	.15*	.29**

* $p < .05$
** $p < .01$
*** $p < .001$

The theory of learned helplessness posits a number of testable predictions. The studies carried out in the Euro-American context posit personal helplessness and universal helplessness as two orthogonal dimensions. However, this was contradicted by Sahoo's (1991) study which showed a significant positive association between personal helplessness and universal helplessness, r (218) = .42, $p < .01$. This, of course, may be a product of culture-specific phenomenon. As predicted, personal helplessness was significantly related to non-contingency and to motivational deficits; personal helplessness was also associated with emotional deficit. This implies that helpless individuals have a negative cognitive set in the form of non-contingency beliefs and they show greater motivational deficits. Helpless individuals also experience less satisfaction in their work place. Thus, the data provided evidence concerning cognitive, motivational, and affective deficits of helpless individuals.

The analysis also showed that universal helplessness did not bear a significant relationship with emotional and motivational deficits. The perception that others are helpless was found to be unrelated to one's own satisfaction and motivation. This was in line with the expectation. Although a significant positive association was indicated between non-contingency and universal helplessness, the association was not as strong as with personal helplessness.

As expected, non-contingency was found to be related to emotional deficit, r (218) = .21, $p < .01$; it was also associated with motivational deficit, r (218) = .15, $p < .05$. The results, in congruence with the expectation, indicated a significant relationship between emotional deficit and motivational deficit. Thus, except the association between personal helplessness and universal helplessness, the associations depicted by the data strengthened the predicted pattern of the relationships that exist between various deficit dimensions.

The analysis was also directed towards examining differences across groups and job levels. It is important to note that job levels in educational organizations involved readers and lecturers, whereas job levels in financial organizations (banks) involved officers and assistants. In industrial organizations, job levels concerned supervisors and skilled workers. Several, 3 (organizational types) × 2 (job levels) analyses of variance were carried out to examine group variation with respect to each of the dimensions.

TABLE 5.6: Mean Scores of Helplessness Dimensions

Organizations	*Job Level-1* *M*	*Job Level-2* *M*	*Combined* *M*
(1)	(2)	(3)	(4)
Personal helplessness			
Educational	26.3	18.5	22.4
Financial	17.6	19.3	18.4
Industrial	25.0	25.1	25.5
All Participants	9.1	8.3	—

(*Contd.*)

TABLE 5.6 (*Contd.*)

(1)	(2)	(3)	(4)
Universal helplessness			
Educational ($n = 60$)	30.6	26.0	28.3
Financial ($n = 60$)	26.1	28.9	27.5
Industrial ($n = 100$)	27.7	27.9	27.8
All Participants ($n = 220$)	28.1	27.7	—
Non-contingency scores			
Educational	28.4	30.3	29.2
Financial	26.4	26.3	26.4
Industrial	28.9	28.1	28.5
All Participants	28.1	28.2	—
Emotional deficit			
Educational	8.5	9.3	18.3
Financial	9.4	8.8	9.1
Industrial	10.8	8.8	11.8
All Participants	9.8	10.8	—
Motivational deficit			
Educational	8.2	6.2	7.3
Financial	7.4	7.6	7.5
Industrial	4.5	3.9	4.2
All Participants	6.4	5.5	—

Note: The maximum scores for each dimension are different.

With respect to personal helplessness, employees of industrial organizations reported the maximum amount of personal helplessness, while employees of financial organizations reported the minimum amount. Employees of educational organizations reported a moderate amount. There was no significant difference across job levels. Of course, there was no significant main effect either for organization types or for job levels. Employees in all these three types of organization reported the same degree of universal helplessness. They also showed the same degree of universal helplessness across job levels.

Employees in educational organizations showed a greater amount of non-contingency than did employees of financial organizations. Employees in industrial organizations also reported greater non-contingency than did employees of financial organizations, although there was no significant difference between employees of educational and industrial organizations.

With respect to motivational deficit, it was shown that employees-in industrial organizations experienced greater motivational deficit than did employees in educational and financial organizations. However, there was no significant difference between employees of educational and financial organizations.

The analysis of the motivational deficit scores indicated that employees of industrial organizations reported the least motivational deficit, whereas employees in educational and financial organizations reported greater motivational deficits. However, no difference existed between employees of educational and financial organizations. Employees in lower level jobs experienced greater motivational deficit compared to employees in higher job levels.

Taken together, the various dimensions were interrelated in predictable ways except the finding that showed a positive relationship between personal and universal helplessness. Personal helplessness was positively correlated with non-contingency and motivational deficit; it was also correlated with emotional deficit. Non-contingency, as expected, was positively correlated with motivational deficit and emotional deficit. Motivational deficit and emotional deficits showed a significant association.

Employees in financial organizations demonstrated the least personal helplessness and non-contingency, while industrial employees showed higher personal helplessness compared to employees of educational and financial organizations. Surprisingly, employees both in educational and financial organization experienced lower emotional deficit as well as greater motivational deficits than did industrial employees. People in lower jobs showed higher scores than people in higher jobs only with respect to motivation deficits. The analysis of personal data indicated a negative association between age (also experience) and personal helplessness and between income level and motivational deficits.

The objectives of this study were to evaluate employees' helplessness in three types of settings namely educational, financial and industrial organizations, and to test the predirected pattern of relationship among five major dimensions of helplessness like personal helplessness, universal helplessness, non-contingency, emotional, and motivational deficits. The findings of the investigation offered several interesting conclusions.

From a theoretical standpoint, the construct of helplessness has been extended to a number of domains such as personality, health, stress, cognition and education. However, its application to the organizational setting was a challenging task. This was possible with an effective operationalization of the construct of employees helplessness. The measure of employees helplessness used in the study offered possibilities for future research in the context of employee helplessness. Although past socialization has been identified as one of the potent sources of work motivation in India, no systematic study existed to quantify the effect. The reported research treated learned helplessness as an end product of the individuals' past socialization and offered a valid method to quantify it, so that the relationship between past socialization and present work motivation could be investigated.

The examination of the relationship between personal helplessness and universal helplessness shows that these two dimensions are highly correlated. This is in sharp contrast to Western findings (Garber & Seligman, 1980) show that the independence of these two dimensions. Although more empirical studies are needed to probe this discrepancy, the positive association of these two forms of helplessness can be considered as a culture-specific phenomenon. The ease with which self is differentiated from others may be low in India; the difficulty of self-others differentiation may have greater spill-over effects. In other words, people experiencing personal helplessness may tend to generalize it to others, people observing others' helplessness may tend to make it a part of their own life experience. Thus, difficulty of keeping experiences of uncontrollability apart may link both forms of helplessness. This is likely in view of our socio-cultural context where dependency on others is greatly stressed.

The previous study (Sahoo & Tripathy, 1990) also showed that these two dimensions are interrelated. While Sahoo and Tripathy administered both the subscales in a single session, subsequent investigation separated the administration of these two subscales by a gap of two weeks with a view to minimizing the carry-over effect. Yet, a significant positive association between personal helplessness and universal helplessness is found, though the strength of association is somewhat attenuated compared to the previous study.

The positive association between personal helplessness and non-contingency and between personal helplessness and motivational deficits shows that cognitive and motivational deficits cohere with helplessness. The association between personal helplessness and emotional deficit adds affective component to the cluster of helplessness deficits. The findings that cognitive, motivational and affective components are interrelated in a predicted pattern amongst themselves and are related to personal helplessness in an expected direction strengthen the efficacy of the theory of learned helplessness. Furthermore, this pattern of findings is revealed in each organizational type; hence it is independent of organizational setting. Moreover, the absence of any relations between universal helplessness and other deficit dimensions corroborates the observation that it is an individual's own experience of uncontrollability that generates bad consequences in the form of a negative cognitive set, motivational retardation, and depressive dissatisfied feelings.

The job level did not emerge as a significant condition in the experience of different deficits except with respect o motivational deficit. Employees at the lower level reported greater deficit; this may be due to the inequitable incentive system prevalent in organizations. But people with different job levels reported the same degree of helplessness, non-contingency and emotional deficit.

Employees in financial organizations showed less helplessness. With this observation, it is conceivable to explain their greater satisfaction compared to other employees. The general observation that employees in financial organizations obtain greater incentives may help to understand the finding. However, the finding that employees in financial organizations exhibit greater motivational deficit compared to industrial employees complicates the picture. The conjecture that the stereotyped activities of banks may have negative effects on motivational strength may be examined in future research.

The findings also reveal that employees in educational organizations experience less personal helplessness and less emotional deficit than do industrial employees. It is plausible that the nature of the activities in educational institutions does not require much decision-making, compared to situations in industrial organizations. The likelihood of encountering uncontrollable situations in industries is higher compared to the educational setting. In addition, educational employees show less motivational deficit compared to industrial employees. This may be a product of the more varied kind of work done in educational institutions.

The major implication of Sahoo's (1991) study is the importance of employee education programmes. It is clearly indicated that the efficiency of employees depends, at least in part, on their perception of control. When controllability is lowered, several negative consequences are likely outcomes. The attenuation of these negative consequences would depend on identifying the negative cognitive set of the employees and combating them. It is also possible to enhance a person's control by imparting responsibility-oriented training and increasing his or her sense of mastery over the environment. Programmes that help employees to explain uncontrollable situations in terms of specific external factors are also helpful in this direction.

In addition to this study, Sahoo and Tripathy (1990) and Sahoo, Nanda and Sia (1995) carried out similar investigations. Sahoo and

Tripathy's study was based on the responses of industrial employees whereas Sahoo, Nanda and Sia's study involved employees from administrative and financial organizations. More recently, Sahoo and Ray (1995) have examined similar hypotheses for military personal (from three wings) in India. The predictions have been supported and generalities have been corroborated. Although these studies do not directly measure employees' output but only scale their self-reported motivational deficit, the support in the direction of the predicted pattern of relationship across studies provide persuasive arguments in favour of helplessness remediation programmes (Sahoo, 2000).

Well-Being

The question of effective coping and general well-being are intimately linked with quality of our life. A plethora of studies have examined the relationship between helplessness and coping with undesirable life events (see Silver & Wortman, 1980, for details). Similarly, Schulz (1980) has provided an elaborate review on the relation between helplessness and ageing problems. Although these studies offer some possible predictions in areas of health behaviour, a few other empirical studies carried out in different contexts such as Indian socio-cultural system may provide insights. Two studies are cited.

Coping Strategies

Patterns of coping are indicative of individual mode of dealing with undesirable events. Although it is very difficult to measure directly the effectiveness of coping, coping strategies employed by individuals can be identified. It has also been posited that direct forms of coping such as confrontative coping and problem solving are more efficacious than indirect (avoidant) forms of coping such as distancing and denial (Lazarus, 1966). Assuming the efficacious nature of direct forms of coping, it is possible to examine the relationship between helplessness and coping effectiveness.

Sahoo and Mohapatra (1992) measured coping patterns of adolescents who were in their early college years. Their helplessness was measured by Students Helplessness Questionnaire (Kanungo, personal communication) described earlier. As with Sahoo and Rath's (1989) study, personal helplessness, universal helplessness, non-contingency, emotional deficit, and motivational deficits were found to be related as indicated earlier. The Folkman and Lazarus (1986) ways of coping scale, adapted to Indian socio-cultural setting by Sahoo, was used. Its strategies included confrontative coping, distancing, self-controlling, seeking social support, avoiding responsibility, escape avoidance, planful problem solving, and positive approval. Considering religion as a major form of coping in Indian context, indigenous items were added to represent religion.

TABLE 5.7: Correlations between Helplessness and Coping Patterns (n = 339)

Coping Patterns	*Correlations*	
	With personal helplessness	*With universal helplessness*
Confrontative coping	–.21**	–.12*
Destining	.30**	.14**
Self-controlling	–.14**	–.11*
Seeking social support	–.30**	–.23**
Avoiding responsibility	.11*	.09
Escape avoidance	.20**	.11
Planful problem-solving	–.16**	–.13*
Positive approval	.17**	.13*
Religion	.14**	.16**

* $p < .05$
** $p < .01$

It was shown that personal helplessness was negatively related to direct forms of coping such as confrontative coping, self-controlling, and painful problem solving and seeking social support. In contrast, personal helplessness was positively associated with avoidant (indirect) forms of coping such as distancing, escape avoidance, positive approval and religion. The relationship with universal helplessness yielded similar, though weak, associations.

The associative deficits found in LH individuals impair motivation to encounter events, try out alternative strategies for solution and explore possible sources of resources. On the contrary, the tendency of MO individual to face events and work out problem-solving strategies are likely to prompt them to direct methods of coping. Although the study was based on the sample of adolescents, similar conclusions are expected in case of general population. This is partly supported by another study which measured several criteria of health including effective coping.

Helplessness and Well-Being

From a view point of comprehensive mental health, the study of well-being is significant. Although the positive association between helplessness and depression has been documented earlier, the question of mental health needs reexamination. There are two reasons that prompt such reorientation.

First, the recent conceptualization of mental health has been changed from a disease-perspective to a health-perspective. While the absence of certain negative life conditions such as depression, anxiety and stress was considered to be a sign of mental health, the present emphasis includes the presence of certain positive states such as personal competence, achievement, and social contact (Bryant & Veroff, 1984).

Second, emergence of health psychology also stresses multi-criteria approach (Winett, King & Altman, 1989). The comprehensive view of mental health includes the freedom from a number of negative life conditions as well as the abundance of certain positive factors.

Prompted by these considerations, Sahoo (1990) developed a comprehensive measure of health behaviour so that the relationship between helplessness and well-being can appropriately be investigated.

Measure of Well-Being

Earlier the measures of mental health available are heavily loaded on one or two specific negative dimensions such as anxiety, depression and stress. With recent changes in the notion of good living, more and more positive attributes such as competence, control, family relation demand a modified scale of psychological well-being. Thus, with a view to including multicriteria measure, a new scale was considered.

Sahoo (1990) has developed a Health Behaviour Questionnaire (HBQ) that includes both multi-criteria features and cultural relevance. Health Behaviour Questionnaire (HBQ) has five distinct parts.

Part-1 comprises criteria relating to health. The criteria include achievement, social contact, control over the environment, feelings of happiness with family, good physical health, job satisfaction, values of spiritual quality, personal competence, social support, freedom from depression, autonomous activities, interpersonal trust, effective coping with stressful situations, integrated personality, and freedom from anxiety. Participants are required to indicate priority ratings against each of these criteria. Respondents are asked to assign 1 against the criterion they consider most important and 2 to the criterion they consider the next most important, and so on. Similarly, they are to assign 15 to the least important criterion. This part of the questionnaire is useful in identifying specific criteria that are considered significant and salient by the participants. The salient criteria are those that are rated first, second and third by the participant. The non-salient criteria are those that are rated 13th, 14th and 15th by the participant. It is important to point out that salient and non-salient criteria are specific to an individual.

Part-2 of the questionnaire consists of 120 statements. Each statement indicates the presence or absence of a health criterion in one's life. The individual is asked to read each statement carefully before indicating the extent to which that statement characterizes his or her life. In order to facilitate responding, a six-point scale is used where '1' represents "very uncharacteristic" and '6' represents "very characteristic" of an individual.

In this part, multiple number of statements represent each of health criteria indicated earlier, but for each criterion the number of statements are unequal. The items representing these 15 criteria are randomized. While scoring, the direction of keying is considered. For every participant, scores are computed for each of the criteria.

Apart from individual health criterion score, overall well-being score is computed by summing the scores of an individual across these 15 criteria. In addition, salient criteria score of an individual is computed by summing the three scores across those three criteria that an individual rates as first, second, and third in the Part-1 of the questionnaire. Similarly, nonsalient criteria score is computed by summing the three scores of those three criteria that the individual rates thirteenth, fourteenth and fifteenth in Part-1 of the questionnaire.

Part-3 of the questionnaire employs semantic differential technique to measure well-being. Bipolar adjectives are presented to denote each of 15 criteria. Numerals from 1 to 7 between each set of descriptions are used. The individual is asked to encircle a number for each set to depict his/her well-being. While scoring, the direction of keying is considered. The closer an individual's rating to a desired criterion, the higher is the score. In this part, score for each criterion and overall well-being score are computed. Overall well-being score (total score) is computed by summing all criterion scores of the individual. In addition, the salient criteria score and nonsalient criteria score are also computed as indicated for the Part-2 of this questionnaire.

Part-4 is the graphic method of measurement of well-being. In this part, there are seven sets of diagrams. Each set contains a human figure and a circle. The human figure represents respondent and the circle represents the condition of good living (a state of complete physical, mental and social well-being). In each set, the distance between the figure and circle is systematically varied across the sets. The distance between the two is minimum at the bottom and maximum at the upper most set. The respondents are asked to examine each set of diagram and identify the specific set that represents his or her closeness to the conditions of good living. For that matter, the respondent is instructed to encircle the number against the set that accurately reflects the distance between him or her and his or her psychological well-being.

The identification of the set is scored on a 7-point scale. The set representing minimum distance between the human figure and circle is indicative of maximum score, whereas the diagram representing maximum distance is indicative of lowest score. The score of an individual is indicative of overall well-being.

Part-5 seeks information such as sex, marital status, age and educational qualification of the respondents.

TABLE 5.8: Mean Well-being Criteria Scores obtained from Questionnaire Measure

Criteria	*MO Group*			*LH Group*		
	Male	*Female*	*All*	*Male*	*Female*	*All*
Achievement	20.78	20.94	20.86	19.77	20.49	20.13
Social contact	31.81	34.08	32.95	31.53	30.19	30.86
Control	39.80	37.16	38.48	37.87	35.67	36.77
Feeling of happiness	43.49	44.54	44.02	42.79	42.60	42.70
Physical health	25.12	23.59	24.36	24.72	24.48	24.60
Job involvement	30.92	30.36	30.64	29.24	27.42	28.33
Spiritual quality	31.19	32.14	31.67	29.67	30.66	30.17
Personal competence	40.90	35.64	38.27	38.40	37.18	37.79
Social support	30.39	32.34	31.37	29.83	29.04	29.44
Freedom from depression	32.18	31.77	31.98	29.62	30.93	30.28
Autonomy	31.95	30.31	31.13	30.21	30.24	30.23
Trust	21.16	21.64	21.40	19.78	20.22	20.00
Effective coping	32.34	30.89	31.67	31.29	30.21	30.75
Person morale	41.75	40.72	41.24	40.30	38.89	39.60
Freedom from anxiety	21.54	20.96	21.25	21.51	20.10	20.82
Overall mental health	65.55	64.82	65.19	63.18	62.14	62.66

The study categorized both males and females into MO and LH group on the basis of median split of their scores on cognitive measure of helplessness described earlier. These MO and LH groups were compared with respect to their scores on criteria of health.

TABLE 5.9: Mean Well-being Criteria Scores obtained from Semantic Differential

Criteria	*MO Group*			*LH Group*		
	Male	*Female*	*All*	*Male*	*Female*	*All*
Achievement	4.39	4.13	4.26	4.14	4.31	4.23
Social contact	4.48	4.64	4.56	3.90	4.18	4.04
Control	4.44	4.23	4.34	3.71	4.23	3.97
Feeling of happiness	5.46	5.55	5.50	5.36	5.64	5.50
Physical health	5.22	4.80	5.01	4.69	5.19	4.94
Job involvement	4.86	4.97	4.92	4.29	4.00	4.15
Spiritual quality	5.16	5.22	5.19	4.76	5.19	4.98
Personal competence	5.87	5.13	5.50	5.55	5.44	5.49
Social support	3.89	3.90	3.90	3.56	3.86	3.71
Freedom from depression	4.95	4.63	4.79	4.36	3.79	4.08
Autonomy	4.05	3.59	3.82	3.97	3.75	3.86
Trust	5.65	5.50	5.58	5.12	5.00	5.06
Effective coping	4.37	3.93	4.15	3.54	3.39	3.47
Person morale	5.41	4.99	5.20	4.84	4.84	4.84
Freedom from anxiety	4.28	4.37	4.33	3.61	3.53	3.72
Overall mental health	72.77	69.68	71.23	66.46	66.23	66.40

The overall picture of well-being supported a marked difference of health in favour of MO individuals. While no significant difference was revealed with respect to a number of criteria, MO individuals relative to LH persons, reported greater well-being in areas of job involvement, social support, trust, effective coping, person morale, and freedom from anxiety. The superiority of MO group was indicated on both the measures (questionnaire and semantic differential) in regard to job involvement. On questionnaire measures, MO individuals showed higher scores on social support and person morale; on semantic differentials MO group indicated higher scores on trust, effective coping, and freedom for anxiety. More importantly, MO individuals showed greater well-being (composite scores) than LH individuals on both the measures. The third measure, graphic design, also indicated the trend in favour of MO persons, though the value did not reach the level of statistical significance.

Parenthetically, it may be indicated that males indicated higher personal competence than females as measured by questionnaire and semantic differential techniques. In addition, males also showed higher control (when measured by questionnaire) and freedom from depression (measured by semantic differential) than did females. The sex difference as found in this study was in line with previous findings (Williams & Spitzer, 1983).

In conclusion, it may be pointed out that helplessness as a general response pattern is not only detrimental to academic and organizational accomplishments, it represents maladaptive orientation for overall life functioning. Since a multitude of criteria associated with desired quality of our contemporary life are negatively related to helplessness, programmes need to be appropriately geared towards helplessness-reducing and efficacy-inducing life goals.

6

COMBATING HELPLESSNESS

The explication of application of the construct of helplessness deepens the impression that remediation of helplessness is a necessity. Helplessness is predictor of depression, disease susceptibility, coping difficulties, old age problems, and intellectual impairment. It is also negatively related to academic performance, work efficiency and well-being. This linkage suggests that helplessness be curbed for an enhancement in the quality of our life.

The remediation of helplessness can be approached from several standpoints. Both the ontogenesis and risk factors are to be considered in the context of combating helplessness. It has been argued earlier that reality (bad situations) in the form of uncontrollable events induce helplessness and insidious attributional styles of internality, stability and globality exacerbate it.

The programmatic research on learned helplessness undertaken by Seligman and his associates has suggested some directions for therapeutic interventions. Since the edifice of the construct of helplessness rests on attributional processes, attribution therapy is offered as a viable solution. However, a few other suggestions have also been offered. These additional remediations include environmental enrichment, personal control training, and resignation training.

Environment Enrichment

It has been stressed that attributional styles of internality, stability and globality are risk factors for the induction of helplessness. In other words, the reality factors play their role in the ontogenetic explanation of human helplessness. Bandura (1977a) makes a distinction between *self-efficacy* and *outcome efficacy*. Outcome efficacy relates to environmental potentials. If the external environment is unresponsive, failures become continuous and uninterrupted source of experience. In such an impoverished environment, the induction of helplessness is inevitable.

Accordingly, Seligman suggests to charge the estimated probability of the outcome. This is possible by changing the environment in a such a way as to reduce the likelihood of aversive outcomes and to increase the likelihood of desired outcome. The changing of objective environment and subjective estimate of the individual's gratification is necessary.

Personal Control Training

Since perception of uncontrollability underlies helplessness, inducing a sense of controllability is helpful in remediation of helplessness. There can be two broad approaches. If skill deficits are real, skill-training is needed for the individual to inculcate a sense of controllability. Bandura (1997) has argued that exposure to masterly experiences builds self-efficacy. An exposure to relevant experiences and remedial training enhances personal control.

The second route may involve perception. There may be perception of deficit. It has been found in the study of the depressives that they demonstrate perceptual deficit even if they do not lack in skills. They underestimate the probability of success. Similarly, LH individuals show perceptual deficits. The reversal of the inaccurate perception is done by exposing individuals to experiential contexts where continual feedbacks are likely to correct their perception of self-skills.

Klein and Seligman (1976) attempted such a technique. Undergraduate college students were exposed to either solvable or unsolvable cognitive problems. Those students exposed to unsolvable problems were then given either solvable problems or no problems. In addition, groups of mildly depressed college students also were given "success" therapy or not. Subsequent performance on a novel escape-avoidance task indicated that both groups given the "success" therapy whether initially depressed or initially non-depressed but made "helpless" by exposure to the unsolvable problems, showed no sign of performance deficit on the subsequent task. In this case, the experience of success is postulated to change subjective perception about the ability of their responses to produce outcomes necessary for successful execution and to avert deficits typically associated with depression and helplessness.

Bandura (1997), in addition to emphasizing the positive role of *mastery experiences* as an effective way of creating a sense of personal control, underlines *social persuasion* as a way of strengthening such control. People who are persuaded verbally that they possess the capabilities to master given activities are likely to mobilize greater effort and sustain it longer than if they harbour self-doubts and dwell on personal deficiencies. However, it is not easy to instil a sense of control by social persuasion alone. Unrealistic persuasions are quickly disconfirmed by disappointing results of one's activities. But individuals who are persuaded that they lack capabilities tend to avoid challenging activities that can cultivate their potentialities. Hence, in addition to strengthening people's perception of their capabilities, counsellors and therapists need to structure situations for them in ways that bring success.

Resignation Training

The intensity of helplessness is greatly proportional to the magnitude of aversiveness or desirability of the events in which individuals are initially placed during induction phase. Hence, the beliefs regarding the implications of events need to be changed. This implies that the highly preferred outcome need to be made less preferable by reducing attractiveness of the outcome. Similarly, the highly aversive outcome need to be made less aversive by reducing repulsiveness of the outcome.

Beck (1970) has found that depressives often have challenging beliefs about the implications (e.g., "If I fail, I am useless"). Ellis (1962) also has similar observation. In order to moderate the tone of implications, people need to be trained to relinquish the extremity of such inference.

However, thrust is placed on attribution retraining in programmes of change.

Attribution Retraining

In essence, attribution retraining refers to changing attributions for failure from internal, stable, global to external, unstable, specific and changing attributions for success from external, unstable, specific to internal, stable, and global factors.

Causal Structures

The first systematic analysis of causal structure was proposed by Heider (1958). As the originator of the attributional theory, Fritz Heider (1958) observed "In common sense psychology (as in scientific psychology), the result of an action is felt to depend on two sets of conditions, namely factors within the person and factors within the environment" (p. 82). Since the early 1950s, psychologists have been using internal-external distinction, but it became a dominant force with Rotter's (1966) classification of individuals into internals and externals. The analysis of causality took an internal-external (locus) dimension.

Subsequently, Weiner *et al.* (1971) observed that some internal causes fluctuate, whereas others remain relatively constant. For example, ability is viewed as a constant capacity, whereas causal factors including effort and mood are variable. Similarly, some external causes such as success in writing compositions is relatively invariant whereas success in rowing is variable owing to the narrowness of the stream or because of the presence of wind. Thus, Weiner *et al.* (1971) conceptualized "stability" as a second dimension. Ability was classified as internal and stable, effort as internal and unstable, task difficulty was thought to be external and stable, luck was considered external and unstable.

A third dimension of causality was then added. Rosenbaum (1972) recognized that mood, fatigue, and temporary effort, for example, are internal and unstable causes. Yet, they are distinguishable in that effort is subject to volitional control; an individual can decrease or increase effort expenditure. This is not typically true of moods or fatigue, which under most circumstances cannot be willed to change. The same distinction is applicable to internal and stable causes. Some traits such as laziness or tolerance are considered as under optional control whereas characteristics such as artistic aptitude is not under volitional control. Weiner (1979) calls this *controllability* dimension.

Two other properties of causes have been suggested intentionality (Weiner, 1979) and globality (Abramson *et al.*, 1978). Intentionality is suggested as a causal property in some respects. A comparison of effort versus strategy explains the dimension of intentionality. One might succeed because of hard work or proper strategy, while one might fail owing to insufficient effort or poor strategy. Failure due to lack of effort meets the criterion to infer personal responsibility, in as much as not trying is carried out, purposively, knowingly, recklessly and negligently. But these criteria are not given poor strategy as a cause of failure. One does not purposively or knowingly use poor strategy. The property that distinguishes effort and strategy is termed *intentionality* (Weiner, 1979). Of course, intent and control generally covary highly. Individuals intend to do what is controllable and control what is intended (Weiner, 1985). But there are important causes where intent and control are distinguishable. Weiner (1979) cites the case of a over-achiever who states that he or she intends to take some time off from work, but cannot control his or her work habits. One might not have intended to kill a pedestrian, but should have controlled his or her speeding. The differentiation between intent and control lies at the heart of the distinction between murder and manslaughter.

Although analysis of causal structures has identified dimensions of locus (internality), stability, controllability, intentionality, and globality, a bulk of the research in the area of learned helplessness has involved the manipulation of internality, stability and globality attributions.

Attribution Therapy

It has been persuasively argued previously that faulty attributions provide process explanation of helplessness syndrome. Both helpless and depressive individuals use internal, stable and global attributions for explaining bad events (failure) and external, unstable and specific attributions for explaining good events (success). Peterson and Seligman (1984) provide evidence to evince this linkage.

On the basis of this theoretical explication, attempts have been directed to use attribution retraining as a therapeutic technique. Often participants in this programme are selected because they ascribe personal failure to less ability. The main empirical finding in these studies is that persistence in the face of failure is enhanced when attributions for failure are changed from low ability to lack of effort (Andrews & Debus, 1978; Chapin & Dyck, 1976; Dweck, 1975), to poor strategy (Anderson, 1983; Anderson & Jennings, 1980), or to temporary external barriers (Wilson & Linville, 1982, 1985).

In attribution retraining, the experimenter and/or therapists directly communicate to the participants the attribution that is desired to be induced (e.g., "you fail because you did not make efforts" or "success depends on hard work"). The participants use information to reach a causal explanation. Moreover, they accept communicated ascription rather than attributing induced failure to low ability. Attributions thus are altered from stable to unstable, which result in the maintenance of effortfulness. The investigators all reported increments in persistence of achievement scorings in the face of failure following the treatment and assumed that behaviour change was mediated by shifts in causal schemata of individuals concerned.

While there is a general agreement amongst researchers with respect to the usefulness of attribution treatment/therapy, differential weightage seem to be attached to various attributional dimensions. While studying the alleviation of learned helplessness in children, Dweck and Reppucci (1973) demonstrated that children with adaptive (mastery-oriented) orientation recognized their *responsibility* in success or failure whereas children with maladaptive (learned helpless) orientation were less inclined to accept the responsibility for their success or failure. Dweck and Reppucci observed that two children may receive exactly the same number and sequence of success and failure trials, yet they react quite differently as a function of whether they interpret the failure to mean that the situation is beyond or within their control.

Many recent studies have been attempted to change this perception of control by 'attribution therapy' (Storms & Nisbett, 1970; Valins & Nisbett, 1972). Moreover, several clinicians (Ellis, 1962) have reported favourable results with patients treated by "cognitive restructuring", "rational emotive therapy" or by modification of "what they say to themselves about events".

In laboratory situation, Dweck (1975) examined whether it was possible to teach children to accept responsibility for failure and to attribute failure to insufficient effort. Twelve children with extreme reactions to failures were selected and were given intensive relatively long-term experiences with a training procedure. The procedure taught the helpless children to take responsibility for failure and attribute it to insufficient effort. During training, relatively easy problems were completed by the students and corrected by the experimenter one at a time. Responses were monitored on the apparatus. In training, failure meant that the subject did not complete enough problems within the allotted time. When the child was subsequently tested, relatively difficult problems were given and corrected by the experimenter in groups of five. No apparatus was used in testing phase. In test, failure meant that the child got the problems wrong. Despite such difference between training and testing phase, children generalized the new attribution (learned in training phase) to testing situations.

Dweck (1975), however, cautioned that all success experience during the training phase would not produce positive effects. Children exposed to "success only treatment" in a second procedure during training phase did not show any consistent improvement in their response to failure. Rather they continued to display a marked deterioration of their performance (in testing phase) following failure. This occurred despite the fact that their performance during training steadily improved. While the success might have resulted in higher expectation of success and might has kept the situation becoming aversive this was not sufficient to prevent the adverse reaction to failure (Dweck, 1975). This observation raises serious questions as to the validity of programmed learning as a success only condition. Programmed learning promotes efficient learned behaviour. It appears that benefits obtained through programmed learning approach are of short-term nature, they do not ensure long-term benefits.

In a different study, Wilson and Linville (1982) attempted to demonstrate that attribution therapy can be successful when certain recent findings in social cognitions are taken into account. First, unlike most previous studies, they attempted to change attributions from stable to unstable rather than from internal to external causes. A major assumption of previous research has been that it is most beneficial to change attributions for dysfunctional behaviour from pejorative internal causes to external factors.

Wilson and Linville (1982) argued that it is more beneficial to get people to attribute their problem to temporary factors than to permanent, unchangeable causes. For example, it will be little solace to tell insomniacs that their sleeping problems are due to the sound of traffic outside their windows, even though this is an external cause, because it is a stable cause that is difficult to alter. It may be more beneficial to convince them that their insomnia is due to a temporary illness such as cold. Although this is an internal factor, the temporary nature may prevent people from worrying about its permanence.

In Wilson and Linville's (1982) study, college freshmen were given information indicating that, on the average, college students improve their grades from freshman to the upperclass years. They were also shown videotaped interviews of upperclassmen who reported that their grade point averages had improved since their freshman year. The effect of this information was significant. Subjects who received this information as compared to subjects who did not were significantly less like to leave college at the end of the first year. They had significantly greater increase in grade point average one year after the study and they performed significantly better on items from the Graduate Record Examination. Although the study provided evidence for attributional retraining, the long-term benefits were weak. So Wilson and Linville (1985) conducted two replication studies. Considered together, these three studies found that attributional intervention improved the performance of college freshmen on both short-term and long-term measures. The short-term measure consisted of sample items from the Graduate Record Examination (GRE) administered right after the manipulation and 1 week later. The long-term measure consisted of actual grades earned in semesters after the study was conducted. The long-term measure also considered the proportion of students who left college in the year following the study. It may be pointed out that the replication studies included self-report measures of participants regarding their future expectation; the measures provided adequate manipulation check of the experimental treatment.

Taken together, the studies open up the possibilities that people may be encouraged to reattribute their problems to an external cause; it would prevent additional worrying and anxiety that exacerbate the problem. The argument is consistent with Weiner's (1974) discussion of attributions about the causes of success and failures. Weiner argues that the stability/instability dimension of causal attribution is orthogonal to internal/external dimensions and that the former type of attribution is critical in determining a person's expectancy about future performance, affect and actual task performance. While a few other studies have attempted such reattribution training, Wilson and Linville's (1982, 1985) studies have the distinctive feature of information exposure instead of training participants. Thus, they claim that as inexpensive, straightforward procedure, it has been both found helpful for people who are concerned about their academic performance.

Despite such claims, some critical issues have been raised in the context of attribution retraining. All retraining procedures assume that some specific attributional styles are faulty. Yet, some critics argue that it is very much context-related. Perry and Magnusson (1989) indicated in their study that mode of instructional condition may determine the appropriateness of attributional styles so far as achievements of college students are concerned. Following failure feedback attributed to ability, effort, or test difficulty, university students observed a half-hour videotaped lecture presented by either a low or high expressive instructor. The three causal attributions affected post-lecture control and achievement depending on the ability of instruction and on students' interpretation (distortion, non-distortion) of failure feedback prior to the lecture. When instruction was poor, the effort attribution produced the best achievement in those students who distorted failure feedback as success. In contrast, ability produced the best achievement in non-distortion students. When instruction was good, causal attributions produced less variability in achievement. Thus, good teaching compensates to some extent for the deleterious effects of some causal attributions.

Despite such moderating effects, attribution therapy has wide range of support. While attribution retraining has mostly been used as therapeutic technique, there are some indications of its preventive role.

Immunization against Helplessness

Seligman and Maier (1967) demonstrate the effect of immunization against learned helplessness. They showed that previous controllable aversive teaching produced a proactive interference with a subsequent acquisition of helplessness when immunized subjects were submitted to uncontrollable aversive experiences. This immunization effect has been demonstrated in various species including humans (Douglas & Anisman, 1975; Jones, Nation & Massad, 1977).

Although an interaction between immunization and attributional style has been postulated (Peterson & Seligman, 1984), its empirical demonstration required experimental manipulation. Ramirez, Maldonado, and Mortos (1992) conducted three experiments to study the influence of attributions in immunization against helplessness.

The first experiment simply replicated the previous study that controllable aversive learning interfered with the acquisition of helplessness. Ramirez *et al.* (1992) found supportive evidence of this immunization effect. However, the second experiment was geared to measure people's attributional style with the help of Attributional Style Questionnaire (ASQ) and to examine whether it has influence on immunization. It was shown that this previous attributional style did not produce any effect on immunization. However, *situational attributions* induced by means of instructions produced effect on immunization. Instructions to induce global internal attributions for explaining negative event produced an enhanced helplessness effect. Similarly, the third experiment showed that instructions to induce specific external attributions produced increased immunization effect. Thus, it was concluded that it is difficult to maintain the influence of a previous attributional style in immunization; nevertheless situational attributions are effective in weakening as well as in strengthening immunization process.

Weiner (1974) underlines changes in person's *expectations* as critical features in achievement motivation. From therapeutic point of view, Hollon and Garber (1980) have articulated a *cognitive-expectancy* theory of therapy for dealing with helplessness.

Expectational Approach

Hollon and Garber (1980) accept Bandura's (1977a) distinction between *mechanisms* and *manipulations*, and argue that theories emphasize mechanisms whereas practice is associated with manipulations or procedures. The authors further hold that Seligman's attributional constructs may provide etiological explication of the process of helplessness, but these do not provide much practical inputs for the remediation of helplessness. On the contrary, the cognitive-expectancy theory, though not inconsistent with Seligman's helplessness model and Beck's depression, offers effective intervention strategies. These cognitive-behavioural strategies focus on expectation—an end product of helplessness.

An Overview

As in cognitive theories, cognitions are considered as variables mediating behavioural responses to events and directly determining the nature and intensity of affective reaction. The first cognitive element is the *perception* of the stimulus event. Perception includes identifying, discriminating, recognizing, and judging objects and events by means of sensory information. As pointed out earlier, there is striking perceptual similarity between learned helpless and depressive individuals. Furthermore, many of the cognitive distortions identified by Beck (1967) as found in depressives are distortions in perception. *Arbitrary inference* denotes the process of drawing a conclusion which is contrary to the objective evidence in the situation. Depressive persons also show *selective abstraction*, a process of drawing an inference only on the basis of a part of information, *magnification*, a tendency to exaggerate the importance of an event, *minimization*, a tendency to underestimate the positive aspect of an event, and *all-or-none* thinking, the tendency to perceive situation in the absolute terms.

The second cognitive element involves the *attributions* made for events. Attributions are simply causes one assigns to an event. Attributions are not automatic process in perception. An individual may or may not use attributions (Wortman & Dintzer, 1978). When individuals do make attributions, the attributions differentially influence subsequent cognitions, affect, and behaviour.

The other element in the model is *belief.* Beliefs do not stand in isolation. They are connected with other beliefs in an organized manner. Its influence depends on its centrality. The centrality of a belief is denoted by the degree of connectedness it has with other beliefs. For example, beliefs about one's own characteristics and capacities, the *self-concept*, play a central role in the individual's belief system. The fourth component, *values*, denote important life goals or standards of behaviour.

Values are evaluative and represent a constellation of several attitudes acquired by an individual.

The major component of cognitive-expecting model involves *expectations*. It is person's subjective estimate that a given event is likely to occur. Bandura (1977a) distinguished two types of expectancy: Outcome expectancy and efficacy expectancy. *Outcome expectancy* refers to the person's estimate that a given behaviour would lead to a central outcome. An *efficacy expectancy* denotes the conviction that the person can successfully execute behaviour necessary for the outcome. Earlier it has been pointed out that those two types of expectancies correspond to the distinction between universal helplessness and personal helplessness suggested by Abramson *et al.* (1978). Hollon and Garber (1980) contend that *expectancy about predictability* is also critical in addition to these expectancies of controllability. The expectancy about predictability indicates a person's subjective estimate that a stimulus event (CS) signals the occurrence of another stimulus event (UCS). Hollen and Garber hold "the notion of controllability typically has implications for motivation and behaviour, whereas predictability has implications for affect" (p. 179).

The identification of these five components (perception, attributions, beliefs, values, and expectations) raise a fundamental question regarding their acquisition. Perception, beliefs and values are basically learned. There is not much information regarding the origin of attributions. Although Seligman and his associates provide some support to show unintended transmission from mothers, evidence is far from being conclusive (see Chapter 2).

According to Bandura (1997), expectancies develop from four major sources: past performance accomplishment, vicarious experiences (social models), social persuasion and physiological states. Cognitive expectations are induced and altered most readily by mastery experiences arising from successful performance. The person assesses and builds his or her personal efficacy. Similarly, exposure to role models provides information what is achievable and what is not. In addition, realistic verbal persuasion by other helps to strengthen expectancy. Finally, the perception of one's physiological states also offers inputs. If the individual perceives greater depletion of energy with smaller amount of work, the expectancy does not grow strong. The magnitude of expectancy is determined by these events surrounding the person.

These various components of cognitions are hypothetical constructs. An attribution represents the way things were, perception, beliefs and values denote the way things are; expectancies define the way things will be.

In any given situation, depending on particular cognitive structures, people may differ in the way they extract and combine information from the environment. Beck (1967) refers to this cognitive structure as a schema. A schema can be defined as a "complex pattern inferred as having been imprinted in the organism's structure by experiences that combine with the properties of the presented stimulus object or of the presented idea to determine how the object or idea is to be perceived and conceptualized" (English & English, 1958, p. 258). Hollon and Garber contend "it is the mode by which the environment is screened, coded, evaluated, and organized into relevant psychological facets. Moreover, even in the absence of immediate environmental stimulation, schemata can channel thought processes. The schemata pattern the stream of associations and ruminations as well as the cognitive responses to external stimuli" (p. 180).

When an event occurs, an attribution may be made. If made, this influences and is influenced by existing belief system. This leads to the formulation of an expectancy about future action and event. The expectation, in turn, influences both motor and affective behaviour. This is the sequence of operation of cognitive components. With respect to depression as well as helplessness, the end result of the sequence includes symptoms of depressed moods, passivity, loss of self-esteem, and pessimism. These various symptoms result from different cognitive components such as perception and beliefs. For example, low self-esteem is the result of internal attribution for negative events (Abramson *et al.*, 1978). Yet, the negative expectations about the future produce much of the depressive symptomatology. Consequently, cognitive expectancy therapy is geared to alter existing negative expectation.

The Cognitive-Expectancy Strategy

The main elements of cognitive-expectancy therapy are drawn from Bandura's (1977a) social learning theory and Beck's (1967) analysis of depression model. The strategy is interactive. It posits that altering any one of the cognitive components would alter other components. However, the efficacy of an intervention at various points needs to be measured in terms of the magnitude, stability, and generality of the change produced. According to social learning or S-O-R model, charging the environment (S) or the behaviour (R) is not an adequate intervention, because the changed response may not be stable over time and may not be general across situations. Although behaviour changes do occur in laboratory as a result of application of Srinner's behaviour modification strategy (S-R approach), the behaviours do not show sufficient durability. In other words, the alteration of cognitive components is advocated as a viable strategy. Now the fundamental question concerns which cognitive components are important to be altered. Hollon and Garber (1980) argue that "the most efficient point of intervention is that which stands at the end, rather than at the beginning of the presumed causal chain, those interventions that most directly impact on expectations rather than perception, attribution, beliefs or values, ought to produce the most rapid and the powerful change" (p. 183).

As pointed out by the helplessness model, a person's exposure to uncontrollable situations might have prompted him or her attribute. If attributions are internal (i.e., "I am incompetent"), this induces passivity. Furthermore, the stability nature of this attribution also shapes expectations about future events. As a result, a person who is unsuccessful in getting a job becomes passive and depressed with the thought: he or she would not be able to get a job in future because of his or her incompetence. The lack of activity further strengthens his or her negative expectation. Thus, the onset of helplessness syndrome is maintained as a part of self-fulfilling phenomenon.

The reversal of this helplessness syndrome requires strategy where the therapist makes intervention. The emphasis is on altering the person's expectations or at least on questioning the certainty with which the client holds that expectation. For instance, questions regarding the frequency and duration of application-making, person contacting and other related activities may be addressed to a jobless person who is hopeless and depressed.

Bandura (1977a) has claimed that *enactive procedure* produces the most powerful means of bringing cognitive change. Accordingly, the existing expectations of the person are to be identified and tested; the person needs to be provided opportunities to "see" the falsity of his or her expectation. It is not the reexplanation of causality, which is central to reattribution therapy, that works; rather the actual disconfirmation of negative expectations via enactive exposure works to produce desired outcomes.

At this point, this strategy may be contrasted with attribution retraining. Efforts directed at altering attributions essentially are geared towards the past. In contrast, in enactive procedure, hypotheses held by the individual are confirmed or disconfirmed by actual observation.

Though direct evidence in favour of the efficacy of cognitive-expectancy strategy is insufficient, indirect support is available to suggest its potency.

Taylor and Marshall (1977) carried out a study to examine relative efficacy of different strategies. In the context of a controlled clinical setting, they compared a strictly cognitive, a strictly behavioural, and a combined cognitive-behavioural intervention. A fourth group provided a waiting list (control group). The cognitive therapy, among other things, included reattribution training as its main component. The behavioural strategy employed situational manipulations and activity schedule to ensure that people have pleasurable and success-producing mastery experiences. The combined cognitive-behaviour strategy used both the procedures. The results indicated that although both strictly cognitive and strictly behavioural strategies yielded better outcomes, than controls, both single focus modalities were outperformed by the combined cognitive-behavioural intervention. There are a few other studies that provide supportive evidence for the cognitive-behavioural procedure (e.g., Shaw, 1977). In sum, intervention procedure that emphasizes enactive procedure to disconfirm negative-expectation appears to be very effective.

The Issue of Desirability of Change

While both the attribution retraining method and cognitive expectancy procedure have been advocated as strategies for bringing about changes in learned helpless individuals, a few critical issues have been raised regarding the appropriateness of these therapeutic interventions.

Although a large number of methods have been undertaken to remediate helplessness (Forstering, 1985), the basic assumption that helplessness is maladaptive has never been challenged (Fincham, in press). Fincham argues that appropriateness of response depends on the context in which it occurs. Fincham cites the case of typical experimental paradigm used for demonstrating learned helplessness. First, performance is measured on a task. Failure experiences are then provided by administering unsolvable problems. Finally performance is again measured. Given to temporal proximity of the test and the use of the same test throughout, it is not clear whether "giving up" or stubbornly persistence is ultimately maladaptive. It is not difficult to imagine situations where stubborn persistence (MO response) is maladaptive.

Correlated with this critical consideration of MO responses is the possibility that LH responses may be a part of coping strategy (Fincham, in press). Specifically, in collectivistic societies, individuals exhibiting so called helplessness are cared for and others come to their rescue for the solution of their problems. With lesser expenditure of time and energy, helpless people get their tasks accomplished. This coping property of helplessness response has been completely ignored by therapists.

Finally, the bulk of the remediation attempts in general and attribution retraining in particular has involved teaching people the value of effort. Although effortfulness is to be valued, various complex tasks encountered in real life situations require other things as well. Attribution retraining emphasizing exclusively effort may not to very useful in the long run. The explanation of several areas of research with respect to the process nature of MO versus LH responses would clarify some of these issues in future.

7

EMERGING ISSUES

The construct of learned helplessness has been offered as an integrative model. It has provided a theoretical framework to guide research in a number of areas of human concern. In addition, behaviour technologists have employed the model to curb certain negative forms of behaviour such as depression and passivity and to strengthen some positive forms of action such as academic achievement and work efficiency. Despite such breadth and depth of the construct, a number of issues remain unresolved. Major issues can be identified at the levels of concept, methods, and remediation application.

The Conceptual Issues

The clarity and robustness of a construct is denoted by the demonstration of its convergent and discriminant validation (Campbell & Fiske, 1959). A well-conceived construct needs to have explicit boundaries with similar and dissimilar constructs.

With respect to the construct of helplessness, these boundary conditions have not been clearly delineated. Although the distinction between personal and universal helplessness brings out its specificity from Rotter's (1966) locus of control and Bandura's (1977b) self-efficacy concepts, there are several grey areas with respect to its relation with other conceptual models.

The conceptual issues surrounding learned helplessness involve *structural, functional* and *mediational* considerations. Cognitively stated, the present research has *structurally* involved perception of non-contingency in general and response-outcome independence in particular. This perception of response-outcome independence is indicative of the lack of relationship between the actor (agent) and the outcome. Although this relationship is postulated to have predictive power to indicate behaviour potential in a wide range of domains, the relationship does not *per se* speak anything regarding the connection between the actor and the other possible means of approximating the specific outcome. The model of helplessness also does not specify the strength of linkage between outcome and each of the contemplated means of achieving the outcome. While proponents of learned helplessness (Abramson *et al.*, 1978) attempt to compensate these deficiencies by proposing and devising a method of internal versus external causal attribution made by subjects, a network of connections with the actor remains clouded in helplessness model.

Connell and his colleagues (Connell & Wellborn, in press) have proposed a process model of perceived control. This is a model of relationship amongst self, context, and action. According to the model, three qualitatively different sets of beliefs are distinguished: (a) beliefs about the extent to which certain personal causes are effective in producing outcomes; (b) beliefs about the extent to which the person has access to the potential known causes, and (c) beliefs about the extent to which the person can produce desired outcomes, without reference to any explicit categories of causes, Skinner, Wellborn and Connell (1990) refer these three sets of beliefs as follows: (a) *strategy beliefs* are expectation about "what it takes for me to do well" (such as efforts, ability, powerful others, luck, and unknown factors), (b) *capability beliefs* are expectations about whether "I have what it takes" (i.e., Can I exert effort? Am I lucky?), and (c) *control beliefs* are expectations about "whether or not I can do well" without reference to specific means.

It is important to point out the similarity between this and the Skinner, Chapman and Baltes (1988) conceptualization. In the Skinner *et al.* (1990) scheme, strategy beliefs are referred to as means-ends beliefs, and capacity beliefs are referred to as agency beliefs (see Chapter 4). The items composing the Wellborn, Connell and Skinner (1989) measure are completely different from those included in the Skinner *et al.* measure. However, the only conceptual difference between the two is that in the former measure, the items relating to causes are self-related whereas in the latter, they are for children in general.

The notion of control beliefs is almost fully represented in the helplessness model in the form of perception of non-contingency between response and outcome. Strategy (means-end) beliefs are partly represented in the reformulated model of helplessness (Abramson *et al.*, 1978) in the form of attributional measures of internality, globality, and stability. However, capacity (agency) beliefs remain fuzzy concepts in the framework of helplessness model. The accessibility of the individual to potential causes is not specified in the framework of helplessness. On the other hand, specific operationalization and dimensionalization of the cognitive expectation both in the Skinner *et al.* and the Connell *et al.* conceptualizations appears to lead to greater predictability in outcome measures. Future research is needed to determine whether or not further dimensionalization of the cognitive expectation (belief system) underlying helplessness syndrome would generate extended predictions in different domains of human activity. It is conjectured that a more differentiated picture of the aspect of helplessness would predict behaviours in wider areas of human functioning.

The other issue concerns the *functional* aspect of helplessness Kuhl (1981, 1984) argues that although quite divergent explanations for performance deficits following a failure pretreatment have been proposed, most theories including Seligman's helplessness model are basically a motivational interpretation of the observed deficits. Kuhl further argues that the degree of *motivational helplessness* affecting the performance of the test task should depend not only on attribution style, but also on the degree of similarity between training and test task. A global attribution of failure to solve the training problem is not a sufficient condition for the transfer of the expectancy deficit to the test task. In a study, a group of students who attributed the failure to solve the training problem to global causes did not show any indication of a transferred expectancy deficit when actually confronted with the concrete test task (Kuhl & Weiss, 1983). Motivational helplessness effects are expected only if training and test tasks are perceived highly similar (Pasahow, West & Boroto, 1982).

Performance deficits following a helplessness training cannot be explained on the basis of attribution style and task similarity. Performance deficits have been found when training and test tasks were as dissimilar as a shuttle-box avoidance task and anagram task (Hiroto & Seligman, 1975). Although such findings underscore the generality of helplessness-induced performance deficits, they do not promote the conclusion that such generalized performance deficits have been mediated by a similar generalization of the reduced expectancy of control.

Of course, Seligman (1975) claims that "men and animals are born generalizers" (p. 36). Yet, the assumption has not been tested directly in most experiments on learned helplessness, although a number of simple rating methods have turned out to be accurate indicators of latent expectancy parameters (Schneider, 1973). Indeed, this assumption has been tested. In an extensive investigation of the generality of various motivational variables, expectancy variables were the most task-specific (Kuhl, 1978). In this study, subjects did not generalize their concept of their ability across various tasks even if pairs of tasks were selected that appeared much more similar than the training and test tasks typically used in helplessness experiments.

Furthermore, achievement motivation research has shown that under some conditions there is an increase in motivation to succeed if prior attempts to solve a task have failed (Atkinson, 1958; McClelland, Atkinson, Clark & Lowell, 1953). This expectation is based on the assumption that the non-attainment of an aspired goal arouses the motivation to engage in substitute activity that may lead to the attainment of a similar goal (Atkinson & Birch, 1970).

Thus, the basic assumption of generalization of a reduced expectancy of control (reduced motivation) from training tasks to test tasks appears inadequate. In a more direct study (Danker-Brown & Baucom, 1982), no reliable correlations were found between the degree of performance deficits observed on the test tasks and variables related to success and attribution of failure. Kuhl (1984) argues that "some subjects develop performance deficits at the test task in spite of a sufficiently strong initial motivation to succeed, simply because they cannot control the execution of their task-oriented intention against competing tendencies to engage in task-irrelevant cognitions" (p. 112). Kuhl proposes a term *state orientation* to denote the inability to form one's attention fully on information related to one's current intention. This construct describes a state of control in which attention is focussed on information related to a present, past or future state rather than to action-related information. In contrast, *action orientation* refers to the hypothetical process of action control; the control is to shield the intention against competing motivational tendencies and to ensure that it would be executed rather than replaced by one of the competing tendencies.

Kuhl (1984) terms *functional* helplessness to refer to failure-induced performance deficits that are caused by interfering state-orientated cognitions rather than by a motivational deficit resulting from a reduced expectancy of control. In the line of his construct of action control, a *three factor theory of learned helplessness* is proposed (Kuhl, 1981). Since the theory is based on the edifice of action control, some salient features of the construct need to be delineated.

Drawing on the ideas of Ach (1935), Kuhl (1984) proposes a distinction between *choice motivation* and *control motivation*. He adds that these two have been unduly confounded in motivational research.

Choice motivation refers to the selection of an intention out of several alternatives, whereas control motivation refers to the actual execution of this intention. According to many of motivational theories, intentions or motivational tendencies can be predicted by an Expectancy X Value model, which assumes that amongst all action alternatives available, a person intends to perform the one having the highest algebraic product of the expectancy to achieve the aspired goal and the personal value (incentive) of the goal. Kuhl (1984), however, argues that the strong intention to solve a problem is not a sufficient condition for success even if the cognitive abilities and strategies necessary for finding the solution are available. Working on a problem requires continuous control of the enactment of one's task-oriented intention against the interfering effect of competing tendencies to engage in various task-irrelevant activities.

The action-control model assumes several processes that are aroused to accomplish an enactment of the intention. The processes include selective attention, encoding control, emotion control, motivation control, environmental control, parsimonious information processing, self-relatedness and awareness. The problem of *performance control* relates to the processes that mediate the final execution of an action (i.e., after the process of action control has resulted in the initiation of the intended action).

From the perspective of this action control framework, the three factor theory of helplessness is presented as a model of coping with repeated failures (Kuhl, 1981). According to this model, the strength of motivation to solve the training problem is not to be confounded with the strength of motivation regarding the test task. During the initial phase of helplessness training, a reactance effect (i.e., an increase in motivation) is expected as long as the subject is confronted with the training task. There is low level of motivation to switch to a different task as long as the subject expects to be able to solve the training task. When helplessness training proceeds to a point where the subject does not expect to be able to succeed, the motivation to continue with training task decreases and the motivation to demonstrate his or her ability in performing a similar task increases.

Thus, initial failures to find a solution result in an increased intensity of the activity previously used to find a solution; this is *invigorative reactance*. Further failures are presumed to result in a process called *action substitution*. It consists of replacing previously used activities with alternative activities that may produce the desired outcomes. The process of looking for action alternatives is called *explorative reactance*. Explorative reactance may facilitate performance during early phases of helplessness training just as invigorative reactance does. A further prolongation of failures is likely to result in *outcome substitution*, a process by which the attainment of the aspired goal is sought by producing an outcome that differs from the one originally intended. The last step assumed in the three-factor theory of helplessness involves a replacement of the goal by an attainable goal that may not be related to the original goal (*goal substitution*).

Several experiments have been conducted to examine this model. Since action and state orientations are conceptualized both as process and as person variable, the experiments included methods to manipulate the degree of action and state orientations and instruments for measuring individual differences in action and state orientation. Kuhl (1981) included a condition in which state orientation was induced by encouraging subjects to examine their thoughts and feelings after they had been exposed to extended helplessness training. Performance deficits (compared to a no-training control group) were found only in this group, whereas another non-contingent feedback group which was not exposed to the manipulation of state orientation did not show significant performance deficit.

In another experiment (Kuhl, 1981), subjects were administered a questionnaire assessing a *personal disposition* towards action orientation or state orientation following uncontrollable events. Subjects were subdivided into two groups on the basis of median split. The experiment on learned helplessness indicated performance deficit in the state-oriented subgroup. Action-oriented subjects even showed a facilitation of performance (compared to a non-pretreatment group).

Branstein and Olbrich (1985) investigated cognitive concomitants of performance changes in an achievement-related context. They maintained subjects' verbalizations of action-oriented and state-oriented cognitions while they experienced success and failure. They analyzed the influence of dispositional action-control and perception of emotional states and personal control. The results indicated that dispositional action-control was an excellent predictor of performance changes that follow failure-inductions. Only a state-oriented group displayed performance deficits, whereas an action-oriented group continued to perform well, using effective action for problem-solving strategies and self-motivating instructions. Whereas action-oriented subjects responded to persistent failure with containing solution-oriented thinking and developed even more effective strategies, state-oriented subjects increased emotional and self-evaluative statements, related failure to loss of ability, and used inadequate solution strategies. The results suggest that the debilitating or facilitating influence of failure inductions on performance is mediated by two different processing styles of action versus state orientation.

Instead of proposing any conceptual explanation of performance deficits following failures, there is also an empirical tradition that questions the validity of expectation generalization. In a series of studies, Tennen *et al.* (1982a, 1982b) and Oakes and Curtis (1982) challenged the assumption that the perceptions of uncontrollability, awareness of non-contingency between responses and outcomes, and attributions made about the uncontrollability of outcomes, are necessary to explain learned helplessness effects.

Specifically, Oakes and Curtis (1982) compared the actual non-contingency with awareness (perception) of non-contingency. The authors argue that these two variables are confounded in experimental studies of helplessness. To disentangle the effects of actual and perceived non-contingency, authors carried out a study. Subjects were asked to shoot a light gun at a target in a brightly-lit room. For one group of contingent subjects, a tone sounded when the light beam hit the bull's-eye. A second group of contingent subjects received a tone when they missed the bull's-eye. Two groups of non-contingent subjects were yoked to the contingent groups, receiving a feedback pattern of tones (indicating hit or miss) that was not contingent on their own performance. A final group (control group) did not participate in this helplessness training task.

Results indicated that non-contingent subjects performed more poorly on an anagram tasks administered at the conclusion of the gun-shooting task than did contingent or control subjects. Awareness of the non-contingency of the feedback was assessed by a questionnaire which asked subjects the extent to which they felt the target shooting task was "double" and the degree to which they attributed their success or failure on the task to experimenter control (versus their own ability, effort, task difficulty, or chance). Feelings of helplessness were measured by asking respondents whether they had felt they could be successful during the target shooting task. Negative mood states of depression, anxiety, and hostility were also assessed. No significant differences emerged between experimental groups on any of these measures.

Oakes and Curtis (1982) conducted a second study to clarify certain points. This study modified the procedure of Experiment 1. In this experiment, subjects received either contingent or non-contingent positive feedback (i.e., a tone sounded to indicate a hit of the bull's-eye). Half of the subjects in each group were then specifically told, after performing the gun shooting task, that their feedback had not been contingent on their performance. This was followed by an anagram task. Feelings of helplessness, awareness of non-contingency, and affect were assessed as in Experiment 1. Results indicated that performance decrements were found only among those subjects whose feedback actually had been non-contingent, rather than among those subjects who were told this had been the case. Moreover, there were no significant group differences on the measures that assessed awareness of non-contingency, attributions or affect. On the basis of these two studies, the authors concluded that a behavioural deficit could be produced without awareness of non-contingency between one's responses and one's outcomes. In addition, they maintained that such deficits are not mediated by feelings of helplessness and emotional distress.

Tennen *et al.* (1982a) report critical studies to examine the relationship between perception of uncontrollability and performance deficits. These authors note that in most learned helplessness experiments, subjects receive feedback indicating a complete failure to control the task. Since there is little variance in uncontrollability, such experiments do not allow the investigator to explore fully the relation between perception of control and performance. The authors conducted an experiment that would permit such analysis. They manipulated the number of non-contingent positive outcomes subject received after being subjected to noise bursts. Respondents were given a box with a button, and were told to try to control the aversive noise. They were informed that a green light would flash when the noise had been successfully controlled, and a red light would appear when it had not. In each of two experiments, subjects in all experimental conditions received 50 noise bursts of equal duration, but received varying numbers of non-contingent green lights, independent of their behaviour. After completing the helplessness training task, subjects were asked to work on an anagram task to test for helplessness effects, and to complete a questionnaire which assessed perception of control, response-outcome contingency, and attributions for success on the noise task.

In the first experiment, subjects who had received 25 green lights during the helplessness training task attempted more complex solutions and performed better on anagram task than those who had received no green light, 5 green lights, 45 green lights, or 50 green lights. This finding occurred despite the fact that subjects who received 25 green lights rated themselves as having less control over the experimental task than subjects in 45 or 50 green light conditions. In fact, among subjects in the inescapable noise conditions, higher ratings of perceived control were associated with poorer performances on the anagram task.

It is conjectured that results are mediated by differential expenditure of effort. Respondents who received 0 or 5 green lights during helplessness training may have experienced little reinforcement for their attempts to stop the noise. If so, they may have been unmotivated to apply themselves to the subsequent anagram task. Subjects who received a large number of green lights may have concluded that it was possible to exercise control in this experiment with little effort and may not have extended much effort at the anagram task. This hypothesis was tested in a second experiment (similar to Experiment 1) where perception of motivation and effort were assessed by asking subjects such questions as to what extent they thought their performance on the noise task was due to effort, how interested they were in the task, or how hard they tried at it. As predicted, subjects who received 25 green lights (non-contingent positive reinforcements) did better on a subsequent anagram test than respondents in the other non-contingent conditions, while still perceiving less control over the task than 45 green light condition. In addition, no difference in self-reported interest of effort ratings emerged between groups. Moreover, neither perceived control nor the attributions made for the non-contingency predicted anagram performance.

Tennen *et al.* (1982a, 1982b) and Oakes and Curtis (1982), on the basis of their studies, conclude that attributions and other cognitive mediators of helplessness are unimportant. However, Silver, Wortman and Klos (1982) view that such a judgement does not follow from the closer inspection of the methodology employed by these investigators. The design of these experiments derived from traditional helplessness induction paradigms by separating non-contingent reinforcement from awareness; some of these alternative explanation of the mediating processes underlying performance decrements are less applicable to their results.

Nevertheless, a variety of possible mediators that can account for impaired performance following "helplessness training" can be considered. Silver *et al.* (1982) list a few such possible mediators. Some creative researchers such as Snyder and his colleagues suggest *egotism* as a possible mediator of helplessness deficit (Frankl & Synder, 1978; Snyder, Smoller, Strenta, & Frankl, 1981). According to them, subjects on the test task try half-heartedly to protect their self-esteem, were failure to occur again. Other researchers (Cole & Coyne, 1977) have found that subjects report heightened feelings of hostility, anger and frustration following exposure to uncontrollable events; this *negativity* impairs performance. Similarly, Coyne, Metalsky, and Lavelle (1980) consider *heightened anxiety* as a possible mediator of helplessness effect. Carver (1979) regards *cognitive withdrawal* as a variable mediator. Since physical withdrawal is often unavailable to subjects following helplessness training, cognitive withdrawal in the form of a mental dissociation from task attempts may result.

In addition to the need of examining the plausibility of these additional mediators, Silver *et al.* raise an interesting issue of probing the matter in an open-ended manner. If subjects behaviours are influenced by tentatively held hypotheses that are not well-articulated by the respondents, such hypotheses, according to them, may be difficult to capture on traditional, close-ended, objectively scored questions. Silver *et al.* suggest that self-statement check lists (Kendall & Hollon, 1981), designed by the researcher to include a large number of diverse and potentially mediating cognitions and affects, might be the best approach when using a closed format.

There are several open-ended formats which have much promise, the instructions to think aloud while performing a mainly cognitive task (Diener & Dweck, 1978; Ericsson & Simon, 1980), imaging assessment during or after a task (Tower & Singer, 1981), video reconstruction after a video-taped social interaction (Klos & Singer, 1981), and projective techniques tailored specifically to the situation of helplessness (Landan & Goldfried, 1981). It is posited that the use of such creative methods may more accurately reveal subjects' thoughts and privately held hypothesis in helplessness experiments, and can suggest how cognitive, affective, and motivational mediators may influence subsequent performance (*cf*, Diener & Dweck, 1978).

Beyond Attributional Style

The foregoing observations deepen the impression that cognitive mediators of helplessness go beyond attributions. Although Abramson, Garber and Seligman (1980) claim that attributions are made "implicitly" or "explicitly" (p. 5), there is little evidence to indicate subjects' spontaneous attributions for success or failure following helplessness training. However, failure to find spontaneously generated attributions among subjects may be due to the fact that subjects are unable to articulate them clearly, or that they may have forgotten their attributions by the time they are asked to report. In contrast, subjects may not have yet ascribed any particular cause for the uncontrollable outcome.

Of course, techniques employed by Diener and Dweck (1978) suggest that, at least among children, careful causal analyses for failure may be rare. These investigators asked children to think "aloud" as they went through a series of difficult discrimination learning problems and then encountered failure. When forced with failures, few non-helpless (mastery-oriented) children focussed on causes for the outcome, and those few attributions that were verbalized did not fit any particular pattern. Rather, these children were task oriented and they emphasized remedies instead of dwelling on causes of failure. Helpless children made "automatic" negative self-attributions for future, frequently assigning causes such as lack of ability. Silver *et al.* (1982) conclude that attributional differences are demonstrated in response to experimenter probes, but free response techniques indicate that helpless and non-helpless individuals may be distinguished by a wide range of cognitive strategies they differentially employ. In other words, the difference is not limited to the attributional variation suggested by Abramson *et al.* (1978).

On the basis of the observation of physical disabilities following traumatic accidents, Silver *et al.* (1982) found that the degree of upset was related to whether or not the respondents focussed on why the accident happened at all. Following Bulman and Wortman (1977), respondents in this study were asked about whether or not they ever asked themselves the question "why me"? Interestingly one half of the subjects reported never asking themselves this question. Those subjects who asked "why me"? three weeks following injury reported significantly more depression, anxiety, anger, and less happiness.

The evidence obtained from this study of the physically disabled suggests some types of cognitions that predict distress. Perhaps the degree to which individuals ruminate about their outcome might distinguish successful copers from those less successful. Individuals who voluntarily or involuntarily rehearse possible outcomes that did not materialize are more likely to report distress (Silver *et al.*, 1982, p. 508).

Another construct that seems relevant for explaining individual difference in response to stress is the concept of schemata. Cognitive social psychologists suggest that schemata are mental organizations of experiences that influence the way information is processed and the way behaviour is organized (Taylor & Crocker, 1980). For example, Landan and Goldfried (1981) point out that how people respond to particular events depends on their semantic schemata (the network of associations to that particular event). Does the word "divorce" evoke "loneliness, loss of income, loss of meaning in life", or does it evoke "an opportunity to begin again"?

Thus, an extensive exploration of cognitions associated with helplessness syndrome is needed to identify all possible mediators. It is also important to go beyond the traditional method of investigation to get around the problem of procedural artifacts.

The Methodological Problems

It has been pointed out that the bulk of research on helplessness has employed experimental method modelled on animal research. Although an in-depth discussion of the limitations of experimental method is beyond the scope of the present goal, it is important to recognize that criticisms have been directed to traditional (experimental) method of study of learned helplessness. Just as certain responses are more likely to occur because of the demand characteristics of the situations employed, some responses may also be suppressed owing to specific experimental arrangement.

In anticipation of procedural artifact, some investigations have been attempted to obviate the pitfalls of experimental method. For example, demands of the situation may be so strong that honest responses may only be revealed to a third party. Aronson and Carlsmith (1968) pointed out years ago the value of separating the manipulations of the independent variable from the measurement of the dependent variable to avoid artifactual results. Under the guise of another experiment, a second experimenter can collect performance data as well as information regarding the mediation process. Since the most important element in helplessness research involves the contention of generality from one setting (training) to another setting (testing), assessment by separate investigators in these two settings would subserve the purpose of limiting experimental bias.

Another front where problems need innovative solutions involves the management of naturalness. Traditional laboratory helplessness studies place individuals in an artificial situation. It makes little phenomenological sense. The kinds of uncontrollable stressors we encounter in real life situations are characteristically different from those that are manipulated in laboratory conditions. Accordingly, findings derived from laboratory research remain inapplicable to many of our contemporary life events. Human helplessness is rarely created by encounters with a string of identical stressors. Instead, people, typically experience a variety of uncontrollable outcomes that differ both in content and magnitude. However, the theory of learned helplessness does not imply that the uncontrollable outcomes received need be identical or even similar. It remains a research question whether performance decrement would be demonstrated if all the outcomes were different.

Similarly, people do not perform in isolation, but rather do so in a wider social context. Others are frequently sources of distraction, interruption, supervision, and criticism. The role of the presence of others may be an issue of consideration.

Furthermore, typical experimental paradigms constrain the range of reactions to uncontrollable events. The test tasks used in helplessness experiments determine whether individuals show performance enhancements or performance decrements. However, as Silver and Wortman (1980) have noted, there are many other ways of reacting to uncontrollable events. For example, they may use intrapsychic coping mechanisms (Lazarus & Launier, 1978) such as denying the implications of these outcomes for their competence. They may also seek support from others, may choose to respond with hostility towards those who are exposing them to such undesirable outcomes, or may withdraw from the situation altogether. Overtly hostile behaviour is less likely to occur in the laboratory owing to the experimenter's position of authority, the subject's role requirements, and demand characteristics of the setting.

There are several possible solutions to the problem of artificiality. Investigators might employ paradigms that more closely approximate real world stressors. Alternatively, they might move outside the laboratory to study a naturally occurring stressors or uncontrollable life events.

In their classic book, *Urban Stress*, Glass and Singer (1972) conducted a number of important laboratory studies on the after-effects of unpredictable and uncontrollable stress. These studies which exposed subjects to noise bursts, shocks, and failure at problem-solving tasks, helped to determine the conditions under which uncontrollable stressors were likely to have deleterious consequences. Yet, Glass and Singer (1972) were aware that this was only a rough approximation to the complexities of urban life. They designed some very clever laboratory experiment that focussed on socially relevant, non-noise stressors like the exposure to bureaucratic red tape and arbitrary discrimination. In one of these studies, subjects were exposed to an encounter with a bureaucrat that was highly similar to the kinds of uncontrollable stressors many of us encounter everyday. When subjects arrived for the experiment, they were shown a memo asking them to report to an administrative assistant of the department to complete some forms prior to participating in the study. Each subject was asked to go to the assistant's office, which was in another building or campus. There the assistant informed the student that each student was required to complete a form requesting background information before participating in any study. In one of the experimental condition, the form was lengthy, and asked for names and addresses of relatives, high schools, and numerous other details. The questions were designed to be repetitious and not to fit into the space provided. Once the subject had finished the form, the assistant examined it. She then announced that since it had not been completed to her satisfaction, it had to be redone. Just as the subject completed the form for the second time, the assistant received a rigged phone call, and spent several minutes discussing a personal matter. After the form was finally accepted, the subjects went back to the laboratory for the "experiment", where various tests were administered to determine the impact of this bureaucratic encounter. The study clearly shows as to how laboratory studies could be designed to represent uncontrollable outcomes encountered in naturalistic settings.

The other creative avenue for the explanation of scientific information is the careful use of naturalistic designs. For example Baum, Aiello and Calesnick (1978) examined an important issue in terms of learned helplessness. They studied crowding and maintained that crowding involves the loss of control over one's social outcomes; repeated exposure to crowded living conditions would produce helplessness. College students were randomly assigned to dormitories with long, crowded corridors or to short corridors where social outcomes were more controllable. Groups of subjects were brought into the laboratory after one, three, or seven weeks of residence. In order to assess the impact of exposure to lack of control, they were asked to perform tasks. An independent sample of dormitory residence were asked to complete a questionnaire after one, three, or seven weeks of stay to assess their mood, and their attempts to regulate social interaction in dormitory. The design enabled the investigators to measure the impact of uncontrollable event (crowding).

The learned hopelessness would state that exposure to uncontrollable stressors leads to an expectation of future uncontrollability; this expectation of uncontrollability produces subsequent effects. However, most of the laboratory experiments on learned helplessness expose animals or humans to a series of small, repeated, and uncontrollable events. Does the theory hold for individuals who experience a single major uncontrollable events such as losing a loved one or becoming seriously ill? Does it affect people's perception of control and their future anticipation of uncontrollability? These questions need empirical investigation. A large number of investigators have studied life events (e.g., Holmes & Rahe, 1967). Yet, as Silver *et al.* (1982) note, no life event researchers have assessed respondent's expectation of future uncontrollability, or subsequent behavioural deficits, after exposure to one or more stressful life events (p. 503).

Operationalization Issue

A related issue in the context of helplessness involves issues of operationalization of the construct. The bulk of the studies of helplessness have involved experimental manipulation with a view to varying specific situational factors such as the length of exposure, or perceived importance of the task, or attributional factors. From a broad perspective, the entire socio-cultural system may be considered as a shuttle box in which individuals experience uncontrollable outcomes. From organizational point of view, the management matrix may be considered as a laboratory administering inescapable shock. In order to study helplessness induced in such settings, it is essential to measure helplessness in ways that are different from task performance in test situations.

As described in this book, Sahoo and his associates have developed and validated measures of expectancy as a measure of helplessness. More importantly, they have devised *projective inventory techniques* to measure helplessness. This method is very useful in the sense that it combines the indirect nature of classical projective tests with objective scoring format of personality inventory. Puhan (1982) has shown the validity of this projective inventory approach. In some socio-cultural systems such as Indian society, there is possibility of test bias in the form of social desirability effects. The problem of reactivity is also another issue to be tackled. However, the projective inventory tests are useful in dealing with these cultural bias (Misra, Sahoo & Puhan, 1997). In projective inventory method, stories culled from daily life are presented. Each story presents a situation of helplessness or non-helplessness. Each story is followed by a number of statements relating to the persons or situations depicted in the story. Respondents are asked to indicate their agreement or disagreement with each statement. On the basis of prior specification, responses are scored to determine the degree of helplessness. Within the format of a single scale, both helplessness and attributional styles can be measured. Sahoo and his associates have attempted this in some of their studies described in this book.

It is important to point out that there have been some attempts to identify LH and MO participants, especially LH and MO children, on the basis of other standardized measures such as Intellectual Achievement Responsibility and Teachers' Behaviour Rating Scales. However, a psychometric measure with demonstrated construct validation is yet to be developed and validated for identifying helpless and helplessness-prone individuals.

Moreover, issues relating to the application domains deserve considerations. It is admitted that the helplessness model has been extended to bring about desired changes in the areas of academic attainments, coping with disease and old age, and experiencing psychological well-being. Yet, research efforts are needed to draw definitive conclusions in some specific cases.

Application Dilemma

By and large, helplessness imparts a negative, connotation. However, the contention that learned helplessness is indicative of maladaptive orientation does not go unchallenged (Fincham, in press). Critics cite cases where persistence against constant failure, termed mastery-oriented by researchers of helplessness, is a clear indication of maladaptation. Similarly, Kuhl (1981), in his analysis of *functional helplessness*, regards LH individuals as successful copers in search of innovative and creative solutions that are discrepant with current solutions. In view of this complexity, there is a research need to determine whether helplessness found in a specific test situation is really a failure of coping or it is used as a solution for improving the prospect of gaining some advantages in other and/or in future situations.

In a typical collectivistic society like India, the label "helpless" may bring some added advantages. When children are perceived "helpless", parents and other care-givers are likely to function as rescuers. These care-givers solve the problems of so-called helpless children. The repeated experience of this external help or the observation of such phenomenon is likely to prompt someone to behave "helpless".

The foregoing argument does not claim that helplessness has functional adaptiveness in all situations. In some situations, it may function as an effective coping mechanism. In other cases, its dysfunctional property is clear. However, the control and remediation of helplessness requires a multi-strategy and multi-level approach. As described earlier, the ontogenesis of helplessness is not sufficiently investigated. Although the role of mother, father, school, and peer socialization has been implicated, the relative contributions of these sources are yet to be determined. It also appears plausible that in contemporary socio-political scenario, the role of leaders, text-books, mass-media in general and television in particular is crucial in the study of the origin of helplessness. More importantly, the medium of transmission and/or influence has to be delineated. Future research programmes in the areas of roots of helplessness and modality of induction would solve the problem of combating helplessness.

Finally, it is important to point out that the model of helplessness appears to have much potential for cross-cultural research. For example, Hofstede (1980) views that people in traditional cultures are socialized to believe and accept the contingencies as finalities without acting on them, or even without making an effort to act on them. In such cultures, people have much higher level of tolerance. Drawing on this observation, Singhal and Kanungo (1994) opine that the people in such cultures may have to experience a relatively higher level of non-contingency to feel helpless as compared to persons in an action-oriented culture where constant questioning and effort-making are accepted as the norms of behaviour as a result of which the learned helplessness would set in rather quickly.

The role of cultural dimensions is further explored in terms of its coping potentiality in different cultural contexts. For example, Triandis (1993) has conceptualized dimension of individualism-collectivism of cultures. Individualistically-oriented societies differ from collectivistically-oriented cultures in specific ways. It would be interesting to determine the pattern of helplessness in individualists vis-à-vis collectivists. The determination of the pathway of helplessness in these two differing societal contexts would be helpful in devising helplessness-reducing and competence-inducing programmes. These are some of the challenging tasks that are in line.

BIBLIOGRAPHY

Abramson, L.Y., Garber, J., and Seligman, M.E.P. (1980). "Learned Helplessness in Humans: An Attributional Analysis". In J. Ganber and M.E.P. Seligman (Eds.), *Human Helplessness: Theories and Applications*, New York: Academic Press.

Abramson, L.Y., Seligman, M.E.P. and Teasdale, J. (1978). "Learned Helplessness in Humans: Critique and Reformulation", *Journal of Abnormal Psychology, 87*, 49-74.

Ach, N. (1935). "Analyse der Willens", in E. Abderhalden (Ed.), *Handbush der Biologishen Arbeitermeth Oden* (VI), Berlin: Urban & Schwarzenberg.

Adler, R. (1971). "Experimentally Inducted Gastric Lesions: Results and Implications of Studies in Animals", *Advances in Psychosomatic Medicine, 6*, 1-39.

Affleck, G., Tennen, H., Pfeiffer, C., and Fifield, J. (1987). "Appraisals of Control and Predictability in Adapting to a Chronic Disease", *Journal of Personality and Social Psychology, 53*, 273-79.

Ainsworth, M.D.S. (1967). *Infancy in Uganda: Infant Care and Growth of Love*, Baltimore: Johns Hopkins University Press.

Alloy, L.B., Peterson, C., Abramson, L.Y., and Seligman, M.E.P. (1984). "Attributional Style and the Generality of Learned Helplessness", *Journal of Personality and Social Psychology, 46*, 681-87.

Altener, A., Kay, E., and Richter, M. (1977). "The Generality of Learned Helplessness in the Rat", *Learning and Motivation, 8*, 54-61.

Ames, R., Ames, C., and Garrison, W. (1977). "Children's Causal Ascriptions for Positive and Negative Interpersonal Outcomes", *Psychological Reports, 41*, 595-602.

Anastasi, A. (1958). *Differential Psychology: Individual and Group Differences in Behavior* (3rd Ed.), New York: McMuller.

Anderson, C.A. (1983). "Motivational and Performance Deficits in Interpersonal Settings: The Effects of Attributional Style", *Journal of Personality and Social Psychology, 30*, 598-604.

Anderson, C.A. and Jennings, D.L. (1980). "When Experiences of Failure Promote Expectations of Success: The Impact of Attributing Failure to Uneffective Strategies", *Journal of Personality, 48*, 393-407.

Andrews, G.R., and Debus, R.L. (1978). "Persistence and the Causal Perception of Failure: Modifying Cognitive Attributions", *Journal of Educational and Psychology, 70*, 154-66.

Aronson, E., Carlsmith, J.M. (1968). "Experimentation in Social Psychology", in G. Lindzey and E. Aronson (Eds.), *Handbook of Social Psychology, Vol. 2*, Reading mass: Addison-Wesley.

Ashton, P.T. and Webb, R.B. (1986). *Making a Difference Teachers' Sense of Efficacy and Student Achievement*, While Plains, New York: Longman.

Atkinson, J.W. (1958). *Motives in Fantasy, Action, and Society*, Princeton, New Jersey: Van Nostrand-Reinhold.

Atkinson, J.W., and Birch, D. (1970). *The Dynamics of Action*, New York: Wiley.

Averill, J.R. (1973). "Personal Control over Aversive Stimuli and Its Relationship to Stress", *Psychological Bulletin, 80*, 286-303.

Baltes, M.M., Mayr, V., Borchelt, M., Moas, I., and Wilms, H. (1993). "Everyday Competence in Old and Very Old Age: An Interdisciplinary Perspective", *Aging and Society, 13*, 1-24.

Bandura, A. (1977a). *Social Learning Theory*, Englewood Cliffs, N.J.: Prentice-Hall.

Bandura, A. (1977b). "Self-efficacy: Toward a Unifying Theory of Behavioural Changes", *Psychological Review, 84*, 191-215.

Bandura, A. (1980). "The Self and Mechanisms of Agency", in J. Suls (Ed.), *Social Psychological Perspectives on the Self*, Hillsdale, N.J.: Lawrence Erlbaum Associates.

Bandura, A. (1982). "Self-efficacy Mechanism in Human Agency", *American Psychologist, 37*, 122-42.

Bandura, A. (1984). "Recycling Misconceptions of Perceived Self-efficacy", *Cognitive Therapy and Research, 8*, 231-55.

Bandura, A. (1986). *The Social Foundations of Thought and Action: A Social Cognitive Theory*, Englewood Cliffs, NJ: Prentice Hall.

Bandura, A. (1987). "Self-regulation of Motivation and Action through Goal System", in V. Hamilton, G.H. Bower, and N.H. Fryda (Eds.), *Cognition, Motivation and Affect: A Cognitive Science View*, Dordrecht: Mantinus Nijholi.

Bandura, A. (1993). "Perceived Self-efficacy in Cognitive Development and Functioning", *Educational Psychologist, 28*, 117-48.

Bandura, A. (1997). *Self-efficacy: The Exercise of Control*, New York: Freeman.

Bandura, A. and Jourden, F.J. (1991). "Self-Regulatory Mechanisms Governing the Impact of Social Compassion on Complex Decision-making", *Journal of Personality and Social Psychology, 60*, 941-51.

Barry, H., Bacon, M.K., and Child, I.L. (1957). "A Cross-cultural Survey of Some Sex Differences in Socialization", *Journal of Abnormal and Social Psychology, 55*, 327-32.

Baum, A., Aiello, J.R., and Calesnick, L.E. (1978). "Crowding and Personal Control: Social Density and the Development of Learned Helplessness", *Journal of Personality and Social Psychology, 36*, 1000-11.

Baum, A., Harpin, R.L., and Vallins, S. (1975). "The Role of Group Phenomena in the Experience of Crowding", *Environment and Behaviour, 7*, 185-98.

Beck, A.T. (1967). *Depression: Clinical Experimental and Theoretical Aspects*, New York: Harper & Row.

Beck, A.T. (1970). "Cognitive Therapy: Nature and Relation to Behaviour Therapy", *Behavior Therapy, 1*, 184-200.

Beck, A.T., and Beck, R.W. (1972). "Screening Depressed Patients in Family Practice: A Rapid Technic", *Postgraduate Medicine, 22*, 81-85.

Bell, S.J., and Ainsworth, M.D.S. (1972). "Infant Crying and Maternal Responsiveness", *Child Development, 43*, 1171-90.

Berry, J.M. (1987). *A Self-efficacy Model of Memory Performance.* Paper presented at the meeting of the American Psychological Association, New York, USA.

Bhana, K. (1985). "A Developmental Analysis of Indian Children's Perception of Control in the Different Domains of School Functioning", *International Journal of Behavioral Development, 6*, 407-421.

Bibring, E. (1953). "The Mechanism of Depression", in P. Greenacre (Ed.), *Affective Disorders: Psychoanalytic Contribution to their Study*, New York: International Universities Press.

Blatt, S.J., D'Afflitti, J.P., and Quinlan, D.M. (1976). "Experiences of Depression in Normal Young Adults", *Journal of Abnormal Psychology, 85*, 383-89.

Booth-Kewley, S., and Friedman, H.S. (1987). "Psychological Predictors of Heart Disease: A Quantitative Review", *Psychological Bulletin, 101*, 343-62.

Branstein, J.C., and Olbrich, E. (1985). "Personal Helplessness and Action Control: Analysis of Achievement—Related Cognitions, Self-assessments, and Performance", *Journal of Personality and Social Psychology, 48*, 1540-51.

Brophy, J., and Goode, T. (1974). *Teacher-Student Relationship: Causes and Consequences*, New York: Holt, Rinehart & Winston.

Brown, I. Jr., and Inouye, D.K. (1978). "Learned Helplessness through Modelling: The Role of Perceived Similarity in Competence", *Journal of Personality and Social Psychology, 60*, 941-95.

Bruner, J. (1983). *Child's Talk: Learning to Use Language*, New York: Norton.

Bryant, F.B., and Veroff, J. (1984). "Dimensions of Subjective Mental Health in American Men and Women", *Journal of Health and Social Behaviour, 25*, 116-35.

Bulman, R.J., and Wortman, C.B. (1977). "Attributions of Blame and Coping in 'Real World': Severe Accident Victims React to their Lot", *Journal of Personality and Social Psychology, 35*, 351-63.

Burger, J.M. (1984). "Desire for Control, Locus of Control, and Proneness to Depression", *Journal of Personality, 52*, 71-89.

Burger, J.M. (1985). "Desire for Control and Achievement-related Behaviours", *Journal of Personality and Social Psychology, 48*, 1520-33.

Burger, J.M. (1989). "Negative Reactions to Measures in Perceived Personal Control", *Journal of Personality and Social Psychology, 56*, 246-56.

Burger, J.M., and Arkin, R.M. (1980). "Prediction, Control and Learned Helplessness", *Journal of Personality and Social Psychology, 38*, 482-91.

Burger, J.M., and Cooper, H.M. (1979). "The Desirability of Control", *Motivation and Emotion, 3*, 381-93.

Burgess, A.W., and Holmstrom, L.L. (1978). "Recovery from Rape and Prior Life Stress", *Research in Nursing and Health, 1*, 165-74.

Butterfield, E.C. (1965). "The Role of Competence Motivation in Interrupted Task Recall and Repetition Choice", *Journal of Experimental Child Psychology, 2*, 354-70.

Caldwell, B.M., Hursher, L., Lipton, E.L., Richmond, J.B., Sterm, G.A., Eddy, E., Drachman, R., and Rothman, A. (1963). "Mother-infant Interaction in Monomatric and Polymatric Families", *American Journal of Orthopsychiatry, 33*, 653-64.

Cambell, D.T., and Fiske, D.W. (1959). "Convergent and Discriminant Validation by the Multitrait Multimethod Matrix", *Psychological Bulletin, 56*, 81-105.

Carver, C.S. (1979). "A Cybernetic Model of Self-attention Processes", *Journal of Personality and Social Psychology, 37*, 1251-81.

Chapin, M. and Dyck, D.G. (1976). "Persistence in Children's Reading Behaviour as a Function of N-length and Attribution Retraining", *Journal of Abnormal Psychology, 85*, 511-15.

Chapman, M., and Skinner, E.A. (1985). "Action in Development/ Development in Action", in M. Frese and J. Sabini (Eds.), *Goal Directed Behaviour: The Concept of Action in Psychology*, (pp. 199-213), Hillsdale, NJ: Erlbaum.

Church, R.M. (1964). "Systematic Effect of Random Error in the Yoked Control Design", *Psychological Bulletin, 62*, 122-31.

Cobb, S., and Kasl, S. (1977). *Termination: The Consequences of Job Loss*, Washington, DC: DHEW (NIOSH).

Cole, C.S., and Coyne, J.C. (1977). "Situational Specific of Laboratory—Induced Learned Helplessness", *Journal of Abnormal Psychology, 86*, 615-23.

Connell, J.P. (1980). *Manual for the Multidimensional Measure of Children's Perceptions of Control*, University of Denver, Colorado, U.S.A.

Connell, J.P., and Wellborn, J.G. (in press). "Competence, Autonomy and Relatedness: A Motivational Analysis of Self-system Process", in M. Gunner and A. Sroute (Eds.), *Minnesota Symposium on Child Psychology, 23*, Hillsdale, N.J.: Erlbum.

Coppersmith, S. (1967). *The Antecedents of Self-esteem*, San Francisco: Freeman.

Cotton, M.M., and Smith, G.M. (1990). "Prenatal Stress and Learned Helplessness", *Australian Journal of Psychology, 42(1)*, 47-55.

Coyne, J.C., Metalsky, G.I., and Lavelle, T.L. (1980). "Learned Helplessness as Experimenter Induced Failure and Its Alleviation with Attentional Redevelopment", *Journal of Abnormal Psychology, 89*, 350-57.

Crandall, V.C. (1973). *Differences in Parental Antecedents of Internal-External Control in Children and in Young Adulthood*, Paper presented at the meetings of the American Psychological Association, Montreal.

Crandall, V.C., and Rabson, A. (1960). "Children's Repetition Choices in an Intellectual Achievement Situation following Success and Failure", *Journal of Genetic Psychology, 97*, 161-68.

Danker-Brown, P. & Baucom, D.H. (1982). "Cognitive Influences on the Development of Learned Helplessness", *Journal of Personality and Social Psychology, 43*, 793-801.

Das, J. (1989). *The Role of Child Rearing Practices in the Development of Children's Helplessness.* Unpublished doctoral dissertation, Psychology department, Utkal University, Bhubaneswar, India.

Diener, C.L. and Dweck, C.S. (1978). "An Analysis of Learned Helplessness: Continuous Changes in Performance, Strategy, and Achievement Cognitions following Failure", *Journal of Personality and Social Psychology, 36*, 451-62.

Diener, C.J., and Dweck, C.S. (1980). "An Analysis of Learned Helplessness: The Processing of Success", *Journal of Personality and Social Psychology, 39*, 940-50.

Digman, J.M. (1963). "Principal Dimensions of Child Personality as Inferred from Teacher Judgements", *Child Development, 34*, 43-60.

Donlon, T.F., Ekstrom, R.B., and Lockheed, M. (1976). *Comparing the Sexes on Achievement Items of Varying Context.* Paper presented at the meeting of the American Psychological Associations, Washington, D.C.

Douglas, D., and Anisman, H. (1975). "Helplessness or Expectation Incongruency: Effects of Aversive Stimulation on Subsequent Performance", *Journal of Experimental Psychology: Human Perception and Performance, 1*, 411-17.

Dweck, C.S. (1975). "The Role of Expectations and Attributions in the Alteration of Learned Helplessness", *Journal of Personality and Social Psychology, 31*, 674-85.

Dweck, C.S. (1986). "Motivational Process Affecting Learning", *American Psychologist, 41*, 1040-48.

Dweck, C.S. and Bush, E.S. (1976). "Sex Difference in Learned Helplessness: I, Differential Debilitation with Peer and Adult Evaluators", *Developmental Psychology, 12*, 147-56.

Dweck, C.S., Davidson, W., Nelson, S., and Enna, B. (1978). "Sex Differences in Learned Helplessness: II. The Contingencies of Evaluation Feedback in the Classroom and III. An Experimental Analysis", *Developmental Psychology, 14*, 268-76.

Dweck, C.S., and Gilliard, D. (1975). "Expectancy Statements as Determinator of Reactions to Failure: Sex Difference in Persistence and Expectancy Change", *Journal of Personality and Social Psychology, 32*, 1077-84.

Dweck, C.S., Goetz, T.E., and Strauss, N. (1980). "Sex Differences in Learned Helplessness: IV. An Experimental and Naturalistic Study of Failure Generalization and Its Mediators", *Journal of Personality and Social Psychology, 38*, 441-52.

Dweck, C.S., and Licht, B.G. (1980). "Learned Helplessness and Intellectual Achievement", in J. Garber and M.E.P. Seligman (Eds.), *Learned Helplessness: Theory and Application*, (pp. 197-221), New York: Academic Press.

Dweck, C.S., and Reppucci, N.D. (1973). "Learned Helplessness and Reinforcement Responsibility in Children", *Journal of Personality and Social Psychology, 25*, 109-16.

Earn, B., and Sobol, M. (1983). *A Categorical Analysis of Children's Attributions for Social Experience.* Paper presented at the annual meeting of the Canadian Psychological Association, Winnipeg.

Eisenberger, R., Kaplan, R.M., and Singer, R.D. (1974). "Decremental and Nondecremental Effects of Noncontingent Social Approval", *Journal of Personality and Social Psychology, 30*, 716-22.

Eisendrath, R.M. (1969). "The Role of Grief and Fear in the Death of Kidney Transplant Patients", *American Journal of Psychiatry, 126*, 381-87.

Ellis, A. (1962). *Reason and Emotion in Psychotherapy*, New York: Stuart.

English, H.B., and English, A.C. (1958). *A Comprehensive Dictionary of Psychological and Psycho-analytic Terms: A Guide to Usage*, New York: McKay.

Epstein, Y.M., and Karlin, R.A. (1974). "Effects of Acute Experimental Crowding", *Journal of Personality and Social Psychology, 15*, 34-53.

Ericsson, K.A., and Simon, H.A. (1980). "Verbal Reports as Data", *Psychological Review, 87*, 215-51.

Etaugh, C., and Harlow, H. (1973). *School Attitudes and Performance of Elementary School Children as Related to Teacher's Sex and Behavior.* Paper presented at the meeting of the Society for Research in Child Development, Philadelphia, U.S.A.

Fennema, E., and Sherman, J. (1977). "Sex Related Differences in Mathematics Achievement, Spatial Visualization, and Effective Factors", *American Educational Research Journal, 14*, 51-71.

Fincham, F.D. (in press). "Children's Reactions to Failure: Implications for Education", *European Journal of Psychology of Education.*

Fincham, F.D., and Cain, M. (1984). *The Pupils Behavior Checklist.* Unpublished manuscript, University of Illinois, Champaign, Illionis, U.S.A.

Fincham, F.D., Diener, C.I., and Hokoda, A. (1987). "Attributional Style and Learned Helplessness: Relationship to the Use of Causal

Schemata and Depressive Symptoms in Children", *British Journal of Social Psychology, 26*, 1-7.

Fincham, F.D., Hokoda, A., and Sanders, R. Jr. (in press). "Learned Helplessness, Test Anxiety and Academic Achievement: A Longitudinal Analysis", *Child Development.*

Firth, J., and Brewin, C. (1982). "Attributions and Recovery from Depression: A Preliminary Study using Cross-legged Correctional Analysis", *British Journal of Clinical Psychology, 21*, 229-30.

Flammer, A. (1993). "Development of Analysis of Control Beliefs", in Johann Jacobs Foundations conference on *Self-efficacy in Adaptation of Youth to Changing Societies*, Johann Foundation Communication Centre, Marback, Germany.

Flanagam, J.C., Davis, F.M., Dally, J.T., Shayloft, M.F., Ony Goldberg, I. and Neyman, C.A. Jr. (1964). *The American High School Student*, Pittsburgh, U.S.A., University of Pittsburgh.

Folkman, S. and Lazarus, R.S. (1986). *The Ways of Coping Scale.*

Forstering, F. (1985). "Attributional Retraining: A Review", *Psychological Bulletin, 98*, 495-582.

Fowler, J.W., and Peterson, P.I. (1981). "Increasing Reading Persistence and Altering Attributional Style of Learned Helpless Children", *Journal of Educational Psychology, 73*, 251-60.

Frankelstein, N.W., and Ramey, C.T. (1977). "Learning to Control the Environment in Infancy", *Child Development, 48*, 806-19.

Frankl, A., and Snyder, M.L. (1978). "Peer Nomination following Unsolvable-problems: Learned Helplessness or Egotism?", *Journal of Personality and Social Psychology, 36*, 1415-23.

Friedman, H.S., and Booth-Kewley, S. (1988). "Validity of the Type of Construct: A Reprise", *Psychological Bulletin, 104*, 381-84.

Garber, J. and Seligman, M.E.P. (Eds.) (1980). *Human Helplessness: Theory and Applications*, New York: Academic Press.

Geer, J., Davison, G.C., and Gatchel, R.J. (1970). "Reduction of Stress in Human through Non-veridical Perceived Control of Aversive Stimulation", *Journal of Personality and Social Psychology, 16*, 731-88.

Geer, J.H., and Maisel, E. (1972). "Evaluating the Effects of the Prediction-control Confound", *Journal of Personality and Social Psychology, 23*, 314-19.

Glass, D.C., and Carver, C.S. (1980). "Helplessness and the Coronary-prone Personality", in J. Garber and M.E.P. Seligman (Ed.), *Human Helplessness: Theory and Applications* (pp. 223-43), New York: Academic Press.

Glass, D.C., and Singer, J.E. (1972). *Urban Stress: Experiments on Noise and Social Stressors*, New York: Academic Press.

Glass, D.C., Singer, J.E., Leonard, H.S., Krantz, D., Cohen, S. and Cummings, H. (1973). "Perceived Control of Aversive Stimulation and the Reduction of Stress Responses", *Journal of Personality, 41*, 577-95.

Goetz, T., and Dweck, C.S. (1980). "Learned Helplessness in Social Situation", *Journal of Personality and Social Psychology, 39*, 246-55.

Goldfried, M.R. (1980). "Toward the Delineation of Therapeutic Change Principles", *American Psychologist, 35*, 991-99.

Golin, S., Sweeney, P.D., and Shaeffer, D.E. (1981). "The Causality of Causal Attributions in Depression: A Cross-legged Panel Correlation Analysis", *Journal of Abnormal Psychology, 90*, 14-22.

Goodnow, J.J., Cashmore, J., Cotton, S., Knight, R. (1984). "Mothers' Developmental Time Tables in Two Cultural Groups", *International Journal of Psychology, 19*, 193-205.

Griffiths, M. (1977). "Effects of Non-contingent Success and Failure in Mood and Performance", *Journal of Personality, 45*, 442-57.

Gurin, P., Gurin, G., Lao, R.C. and Beattie, M. (1969). "Internal-external Control in the Motivational Dynamics of Negro Youth, *Journal of Social Issues, 25*, 29-53.

Hackman, J.R. and Pearce, J.L., and Wolfe, J.C. (1978). "Effects of Changes in Job Characteristics on Work Attitudes and Behaviour: A Naturally Occurring Quasi-experiment", *Organizational Behaviour and Human Performance, 21*, 289-304.

Hanusa, B.H., and Schulz, R. (1977). "Attributional Mediators of Learned Helplessness", *Journal of Personality and Social Psychology, 85*, 577-86.

Heckhausen, H. (1982). "The Development of Achievement Motivation", in W.W. Hartup (Ed.), *Review of Child Development Research* (pp. 600-68), Chicago: University of Chicago Press.

Heider, F. (1958). *The Psychology of Interpersonal Relation*, New York: Wiley.

Hess, R., Kashigawi, K., Azuma, H., Price, G.G. and Dickson, W. (1980). "Maternal Expectation for Early Mastery of Developmental Tasks and Cognitive and Social Competence of Preschool Children in Japan and the United States", *International Journal of Psychology, 15*, 259-71.

Hill, K.T. and Sarason, S.B. (1966). "The Relation of Test Anxiety and Defensiveness to Test and School Performance over the Elementary

School Years: A Further Longitudinal Study", *Monographs of the Society for Research in Child Development*, Serial No. 104, *31*, (Whole No. 2).

Hilton, T.L., and Berglund, G.W. (1974). "Sex Differences in Mathematics Achievement—A Longitudinal Study", *Journal of Education Research, 67*, 231-37.

Hiroto, D.S. (1974). "Locus of Control and Learned Helplessness", *Journal of Experimental Psychology, 102*, 187-93.

Hiroto, D.S., and Seligman, M.E.P. (1975). "Generality of Learned Helplessness in Man", *Journal of Personality and Social Psychology, 31*, 331-27.

Hofstede, G. (1980). *Culture's Consequences: International Differences in Work-related Values*, London: Sage.

Hokoda, A., and Fincham, F.D. (1995). "Origins of Children's Helpless and Mastery Achievement Patterns in the Family", *Journal of Educational Psychology, 87*, 375-85.

Hollon, S.D., and Garber, T. (1980). "A Cognitive Expectancy Theory of Therapy for Helplessness and Depression", in J. Garber and M.E.P. Seligman (Eds.), *Human Helplessness: Theory and Application*, New York: Academic Press.

Holmes, T.H., and Rahe, R.H. (1967). "The Social Readjustment Rating Scale", *Journal of Psychosomatic Research, 11*, 213-18.

Hymel, S. (1983). *Social Isolation and Rejection in Children: The Child's Perspective.* Paper presented at the biennial meeting of the Society for Research in Child Development, Detroit, USA.

Ickes, W.J., and Layden, M.A. (1978). "Attributional Styles", in J. Harvey, W. Ickes, R. Kidd (Eds), *New Direction in Attributional Research (Vol. 2)*, Hillside, N.J.: Lawrence Erlbaum Associates.

Jenkins, C.D., Zyzanski, S.J., and Rosenman, R.H. (1976). "Risk of New Myocardial Infarction in Middle Aged Men with Manifest Coronary Heat Disease", *Circulation, 53*, 342-47.

Jessor, R., Donovar, J.E., and Costa, F.M. (1991). *Beyond Adolescence: Problem Behaviour and Young Adult Development*, Cambridge: Cambridge University Press.

Johnson, D.S. (1981). "Naturally Acquired Learned Helplessness: The Relationship of School Failure to Achievement Behaviour, Attributions, and Self-concept", *Journal of Educational Psychology, 73*, 174-80.

Joiner, T.E. and Wagner, K.D. (1995). "Attributions Style and Depression in Children and Adolescents: A Meta-analytic Review", *Child Psychology Review, 15*, 772-98.

Jones, S.L., Nation, J.R., and Massad, P. (1977). "Immunization against Learned Helplessness in Man", *Journal of Abnormal Psychology, 86*, 75-83.

Kagitcibasi (1996). *Family and Human Development Across Cultures: A View from Other Side*, Mahwah, New Jersey: Lawrence Erlbaum.

Kanungo, R.N. (Personal Communication). *Students' Helplessness Questionnaire*, Unpublished report, Faculty of Management, McGill University, Montreal, Canada.

Kanungo, R.N., and Misra, S. (1985). "Declining Work Motivation in India", *Indian Management*, 7-14.

Kanungo, R.N., and Sahoo, F.M. (1988). *Employees' Helplessness Questionnaire*, Unpublished report, Psychology Department, Utkal University, Bhubaneswar, India.

Karasek, R.A., Jr. (1979). "Job Demands, Decision Latitudes, and Mental Stress Implications for Job Redesign", *Administrative Sciences Quarterly, 24*, 285-308.

Kelman, H.R., Lowerthal, M., and Muller, J.N. (1966). "Community Status of Discharged Rehabilitation Patients: Results of Longitudinal Study", *Archives of Physical Medicine and Rehabilitation, 47*, 670-75.

Kendall, P.C. and Hollon, S.D. (1981). "Assessing Self-referent Speech: Methods in the Measurement of Self-statements", in P.C. Kendall and S.D. Hollon (Eds.), *Assessment Strategies for Cognitive—Behavioural Interventions*, New York: Academic Press.

Kindermann, T., and Skinner, E.A. (1989). *Mothers' Perception of Children's Progress in Developmental Tasks: Organizers of Contingencies in Every Day Interaction*. Paper presented at the symposium on the effect of parents beliefs on child development, annual meeting of the Society for Research in Child Development, Kansas, USA.

Klein, D.C., Fencil-Morse, E., and Seligman, M.E.P. (1976). "Learned and Helplessness, Depression and the Attribution of Failure", *Journal of Abnormal Psychology, 85*, 11-26.

Klein, D.C., and Seligman, M.E.P. (1976). "Reversal of Performance Deficits in Learned Helplessness and Depression," *Journal of Abnormal Psychology, 85*, 11-26.

Klos, D., and Singer, J.L. (1981). "Determinants of the Adolescents Ongoing Thought following Simulated Parental Confrontations", *Journal of Personality and Social Psychology, 41*, 975-87.

Koller, P.S., and Kaplan, R.M. (1978). "A Two Process Theory of Learned Helplessness", *Journal of Personality and Social Psychology, 36*, 1177-83.

Kovacs, M., and Beck, A.T. (1977). "An Empirical-clinical Approach Toward a Definition of Childhood Depression", in J.G. Schulterbrandt and A. Raskin (Eds.), *Depression in Childhood: Diagnosis, Treatment and Conceptual Models* (pp. 1-25), New York: Raven Press.

Krantz, D.S. and Schulz, R. (1980). "Personal Control and Health: Some Applications to Crisis of Middle and Old Age", in J. Singer and A. Baum (Eds.), *Advances in Environmental Psychology*, Hillsdale, New Jersey: Lawrence Erlbaum.

Kuhl, J. (1978). "Standard Setting and Task Preference: An Elaboration of the Theory of Achievement Motivation and An Empirical Test", *Psychological Review, 85*, 239-48.

Kuhl, J. (1981). "Motivational and Functional Helplessness: The Moderating Effect of State Versus Action Orientation", *Journal of Personality and Social Psychology, 40*, 155-70.

Kuhl, J. (1984). "Volitional Aspects of Achievement Motivation and Learned Helplessness: Toward a Comprehensive Theory of Action Control", *Progress in Experimental Personality Research, 13*, 99-171.

Kuhl, J. and Weiss, M. (1983). *Performance Deficits following Uncontrollable Failure: Global Attributions and Generalized Expectancy Deficits on an Important Action Control*, Manuscript submitted.

Kun, A. (1977). "Development of Magnitude Coronation and Compensation Schemata in Ability and Effort Attribution of Performance", *Child Development, 46*, 862-73.

Lamb, M.E. (1979). "Social Development in Infancy: Reflections on a Theme", *Human Development, 22*, 68-72.

Lamb, M.E., and Esterbrooks, M.A. (1981). "Individual Differences in Parental Sensitivity: Some Thoughts about Origins, Components, and Consequences", in M.E. Lamb and L.R. Sherrod (Eds), *Infant Social Cognition: Empirical and Theoretical Considerations (pp. 127-53)*, Hillsdale, NJ: Erlbaum.

Lambert, W., Hamers, J. and Frasure-Smith, N. (1979). "Child-rearing Values: A Cross-cultural Study", New York: Praeger.

Landan, R.J. and Goldfried, M.B. (1981). "The Assessment of Schemata: A Unifying Framework for Cognitive, Behavioural and Traditional Assessment", in P.C. Kendall and S.D. Hollon (Eds), *Assessment Strategies for Cognitive, Behavioural Interventions*, New York: Academic Press.

Langer, E. (1983). *Psychology of Control*, Beverly Hills, California: Sage.

Langer, E.J., and Rodin, J. (1976). "The Effects of Choice and Enhanced Personal Responsibility for the Aged: A Field Experiment in an Institutional Setting", *Journal of Personality and Social Psychology, 34*, 191-98.

Laosa, L. (1980). "Maternal Teaching Strategies in Chicano and Anglo-American Families: The Influence of Culture and Education on Maternal Behavior", *Child Development, 51*, 759-65.

Lazarus, R.S. (1966). *Psychological Stress and the Coping Process*, New York: McGraw-Hill.

Lazarus, R.S., and Launier, R. (1978). "Stress-related Transactions between Person and Environment", in L.A. Pervin and M. Lewis (Eds.), *Perspectives in International Psychology*, New York: Plenum.

Lefcourt, H.M. (1976). *Locus of Control: Current Trends in History and Research*, New York: Wiley.

Lefcourt, H.M. (1979). "Locus of Control and Coping with Life's Events", in F. Staub (Ed.), *Personality*, Englewood Cliffs, NJ: Prentice Hall.

Lefcourt, H.M. (1980). "Personality and Locus of Control", in J. Garber and M.E.P. Seligman (Eds.), *Human Helplessness: Theory and Applications*, (pp. 245-60), New York: Academic Press.

Lenny, E. (1977). "Women's Self-confidence in Achievement Settings", *Psychological Bulletin, 84*, 1-13.

Lent, R.W., Brown, S.D. and Larkin, R.C. (1984). "Relation of Self-efficacy Expectation to Academic Achievement and Performance", *Journal of Counselling Psychology, 31*, 356-62.

LeShan, L. (1961). "A Basic Psychological Orientation Apparently Associated with Malignant Disease", *Psychiatric Quarterly, 35*, 314-30.

Lewis, M., and Goldberg, S. (1969). "Perceptual Cognitive Development Infancy: 'A Generalized Expectancy Model as a Function of Mother-infant Interactions", *Merrill-Palmir Quarterly, 19*, 81-100.

Licht, B.G., and Dweck, C.S. (1984). "Determinants of Academic Achievements: The Interaction of Children's Achievement Orientations with Skill Area", *Developmental Psychology, 20*, 628-63.

Licht, R.G., and Shapiro, S.H. (1982). *Sex Differences on Attributions among High Achievers*. Paper presented at the meeting of the American Psychological Association, Washington, D.C.

Litman, T.J. (1962). "The Influence of Self-conception and Life Orientation Factors in the Rehabilitation of the Orthopedically Disabled", *Journal of Health and Human Behaviour, 3*, 249-56.

Little, T.D., Oettingen, G., Stetsenko, A., and Baltes, P.B. (1994). *A Mean and Covariance Structure (MACS) Assessment of the Factorial Structure of the Control, Agency and Means—Ends Interview: A Core Sample Validation*, Berlin: Max-Planck Institute of Human Development and Education.

Maccoby, E.D., and Jacklin, C.S. (1974). *The Psychology of Sex Difference*, Stinford, California: Stinford University Press.

Maddux, J.E. and Rogers, R.W. (1983). "Protection Motivation and Self-efficacy: A Revised Theory of Fear Appeals and Attitude Change", *Journal of Experimental Social Psychology, 15*, 469-79.

Maddux, J.E., Sheer M. and Rogers, R.W. (1982). "Self-effecting Expectancy and Outcome Expectancy: Their Relationship and their Effects on Behaviour Intentions", *Cognitive Theory and Research, 6*, 207-11.

Mandler, G. (1972). "Helplessness: Theory and Research in Anxiety", in C.D. Spielberger (Ed.), *Anxiety: Current Trends in Theory and Research*, New York: Academic Press.

Mandler, G., and Watson, D.L. (1966). "Anxiety and Interruption of Behaviour", in C.D. Spielberger (Ed.), *Anxiety and Behavior*, New York: Academic Press.

Matthews, K.A. (1988). "Coronary Heart Disease and Type A Behaviour: Update on and Alternative to the Booth-Kewley and Friedman (1967) Quantitative Review", *Psychological Bulletin, 194*, 373-80.

McCandless, B., Roberts, A., Starnes, T. (1972). "Teachers' Marks Achievement Test Scores and Aptitude Relation with Respect to Social Class, Race, and Sex", *Journal of Educational Psychology, 63*, 153-59.

McClelland, D.C. (1961). *The Achieving Society*, Princeton: Van Nostrand.

McClelland, D.C., Atkinson, J.W., Clark, R.A. and Lowell, E.L. (1953) (Eds.), *The Achievement Motive*, New York: Appleton.

McFerland, C. and Ross, M. (1982). "Impact of Causal Attribution on Affective Reactions to Success and Failure", *Journal of Personality and Social Psychology, 43*, 612-17.

McKegney, F. and Lange, P. (1971). "The Decision to no Longer Live on Chronic Dialysis", *American Journal of Psychiatry, 126*, 167.

McMahan, I. (1973). "Relationship between Causal Attribution and Experiences of Success", *Journal of Personality and Social Psychology, 28*, 108-14.

Miller, L.W., and Norman, W.H. (1979). "Learned Helplessness in Humans: A Review and Attribution Theory Model", *Psychological Bulletin, 60*, 93-119.

Miller, W.R., and Seligman, M.E.P. (1973). "Depression and Learned Helplessness in Man", *Journal of Abnormal Psychology, 82*, 62-73.

Misra, G., Sahoo, F.M., and Puhan, B.N. (1997). "Cultural Bias in Testing: India", *European Review of Applied Psychology, 47(4)*, 309-16.

Montanelli, D.S., and Hill, K.T. (1969). "Children's Achievement Expectations and Performance as a Function of Two Consecutive Reinforcement, Sex of Subject, and Sex of Experimenter", *Journal of Personality and Social Psychology, 31*, 369-99.

Moss, H.A., and Jones, S.T. (1977). "Relations between Maternal Attitude and Maternal Behaviour as a Function of Social Class", in P.H. Zeidermann, S.R. Tulkin, and H. Rosenfeld (Eds.), *Culture and Infancy*, New York: Academic Press.

Moulton, K.D., Brown, S.D. and Lent, R.W. (1991). "Relation of Self-efficacy Beliefs to Academic Outcomes: A Meta-analytic Investigation", *Journal of Counselling Psychology, 18*, 30-38.

Naditch, M.P. (1974). "Locus of Control, Discontent, and Hypertension", *Social Psychiatry, 9*, 111-17.

Naditch, M.P., Gargan, M.A., and Michael, L.B. (1975). "Denial, Anxiety, Locus of Control and the Discrepancy between Aspirations and Achievements as Components of Depression", *Journal of Abnormal Psychology, 84*, 1-9.

Navarra, A. (1981). *Unpublished Report*, University of Pennsylvania, Philadelphia, U.S.A.

Nicholls, J.G. (1975). "Causal Attributions and Other Achievement Related Cognitions: Effects of Task Outcome, Attainment Value and Sex", *Journal of Personality and Social Psychology, 31*, 379-89.

Nicholls, J.G. (1978). "The Development of the Concepts of Effort and Ability; Perception of Academic Attainment, and the Understanding that Difficult Task Require More Ability", *Child Development, 49*, 800-14.

Ninio, A. (1979). "The Naïve Theory of the Infant and Other Maternal Attitudes in Two Subgroups in Israel", *Child Development, 50*, 976-80.

Nolen-Hoeksema, S., Girgus, J.S., and Seligman, M.E.P. (1986). "Learned Helplessness in Children: A Longitudinal Study of Depression, Achievement, and Explanatory Style", *Journal of Personality and Social Psychology, 51*, 435-42.

Oakes, W.F., and Curtis, N. (1982). "Learned Helplessness: Not Dependent on Cognitive Attributions or Other Such Phenomenal Experiences", *Journal of Personality*, 1982, 30, 387-405.

Overmier, J.B. and Seligman, M.E.P. (1967). "Effects of Inescapable Shock upon Subsequent Escape and Avoidant Learning", *Journal of Comparative and Physiological Psychology, 63*, 28-33.

Paikray, P., and Sahoo F.M. (1994). *Child-rearing Antecedents of Children's Learned Helplessness*. Unpublished report, Psychology Department, Utkal University, Bhubaneswar, India.

Parke, R.D. (1978). "Parent Infant Interaction? Progress, Paradigms, and Problems", in G. Sackett (Ed.), *Observing Behaviour (Vol. 1): Theory and Application in Mental Retardation*, Baltimore, Maryland: University Park Press.

Parke, R.D., Hymel, S., Power, T.G., and Tinsly, B.R. (1980). "Fathers and Risk: A Hospital Based Model of Intervention", in L.O. Walker, and J.H. Pentiwff (Eds.), *Exceptional Infant* (Vol. 4), New York: Brunner/Mazel.

Pasahow, R.J. (1980). "The Relation between An Attributional Dimension and Learned Helplessness", *Journal of Abnormal Psychology, 89*, 358-67.

Pasahow, R.J., West, S.G., and Boroto, D.R. (1982). "Predicting When Uncontrollability will Produce Performance Deficits: A Refinement of the Reformulated Learned Helplessness Hypothesis", *Psychological Review, 89*, 595-98.

Perry, R.P., and Magnusson, J.L. (1989). "Causal Attributions and Perceived Performance: Consequences for College Students, Achievement and Perceived Control in Different Instructional Conditions", *Journal of Educational Psychology, 81*, 164-72.

Peterson, C., Bettes, B.A., and Seligman, M.E.P. (1982). *Spontaneous Attributions and Depressive Symptoms*. Unpublished manuscript, Virginia Polytechnic Institute and State University, Virginia, U.S.A.

Peterson, C., and Seligman, M.E.P. (1981). "Helplessness and Attribution Style in Depression", *Tiddsskrift for Norsk Psykologforsia, 18*, 3-18: 53-59.

Peterson, C., and Seligman, M.E.P. (1983). "Learned Helplessness and Victimization", *Journal of Social Issues, 2*, 103-16.

Peterson, C., and Seligman, M.E.P. (1984). "Causal Explanation as a Risk Factor for Depression: Theory and Evidence", *Psychological Review, 91*, 347-74.

Peterson, C., Semmel, A., VonBaeyer, C., Abramson, L.Y., Metalsky, G.I., and Seligman, M.E.P. (1982). "The Attributional Style Questionnaire", *Cognitive Therapy and Research, 6*, 287-99.

Phares, E.J. (1976). *Locus of Control in Personality*, Morristown, NJ: General Learning Press.

Piaget, J. (1936). *The Origins of Intelligence in the Child*, New York: International University Press.

Piori, M., Garino, E., Samson, A. and Oberklaid, F. (1986). "Ethnic Differences on Difficult Temperament and Behaviour Problems in Children". Paper presented at the 8th International Conference on Cross-Cultural Psychology, Istanbul, Turkey.

Puhan, B.N. (1982). *Psychometric Issues in Measurement*, Agra: National Psychological Corporation.

Ramey, C.T., and Finkelstein, N.W. (1978). "Contingent Stimulation and Infant Competence", *Journal of Pediatric Psychology, 3*, 89-96.

Ramey, C.T., Starr, R.H., Pallas, J., Whitten, C.F., and Reed, V. (1975). "Nutrition Response Contingent Stimulation and the Maternal Deprivation Syndrome: Results of an Early Intervention Program", *Merrill-Palmer Quarterly, 21*, 45-53.

Ramirez, E., Maldonado, A., and Mortos, R. (1992). "Attributions Modulate Immunization against Learned Helplessness in Humans", *Journal of Personality and Social Psychology, 62*, 1-9.

Raps, C.S., Peterson, C., Jonas, M., and Seligman, M.E.P. (1982). "Patient Behavior in Hospitals: Helplessness, Reactance, or Both?" *Journal of Personality and Social Psychology, 42*, 1036-41.

Raps, C.S., Peterson, C., Reinhart, K.E., Abramson, L.Y., and Seligman, M.E.P. (1982). "Attributional Style Among Depressed Patients", *Journal of Abnormal Psychology, 91*, 102-08.

Reim, B., Glass, D.C., and Singer, J.E. (1971). "Behavioral Consequences of Exposure to Uncontrollable and Unpredictable Noise", *Journal of Applied Social Psychology, 1*, 44-56.

Rholer, W.S., Blackwell, J., Jordan, C., and Walters, C. (1980). "A Developmental Study of Learned Helplessness", *Developmental Psychology, 16*, 616-24.

Riksen-Walraven, T. (1978). "Effects of Caregiver Behaviour on Habituation Rate and Self-efficacy in Infants", *International Journal of Behavioural Development, 1*, 105-30.

Rizley, R. (1978). "Depression and Distortion in the Attribution of Causality", *Journal of Abnormal Psychology, 87*, 32-48.

Rodin, J., and Langer, E.J. (1977). "Long-term Effects of a Control-relevant Intervention with the Institutionalised Aged", *Journal of Personality and Social Psychology, 35*, 897-902.

Rosenbaum, M., and Ben-Ari, K. (1985). "Learned Helplessness and Learned Resourcefulness: Effects of Noncontingent Success and Failure on Individuals Differing in Self-control Skills", *Journal of Personality and Social Psychology, 35*, 198-215.

Rosenbaum, R.M. (1972). *Dimensional Analysis of the Perceived Causes of Success and Failure.* Unpublished Doctoral Dissertation, University of California, Los Angeles.

Rosenman, R.H., Brand, R.J., Jenkins, C.D., Fridman, M., Straus, R., and Wurm, M. (1975). "Coronary Heart Disease in the Western Collaborative Group Study: Final Follow-up Experience of 8½ years", *Journal of the American Medical Association, 233*, 872-77.

Rosenman, R.H., Friedman, M., Strauss R., Warm M., Kositcher, R., Hahn W., and Werthesan, N.T. (1964). "A Predictive Study of Coronary Heart Disease", *Journal of American Medical Association, 189*, 15-22.

Rosenthal, D.A., and Bornholt, L. (1987). *Cultural Variations in Child-rearing Practices.* Unpublished manuscript, University of Melbourne, Australia.

Rosenthal, D.A., and Bornholt, L. (1988). "Expectations about Development in Greek and Anglo-Australian Families", *Journal of Cross-Cultural Psychology, 19*, 19-34.

Rosenthal, R., and Jacobson, L. (1968). *The Pygmalion in the Classroom*, New York: Holt, Rinehart & Winston.

Roth, S., and Kubal, L. (1975). "Effects of Non-contingent Reinforcement on Tasks of Differing Importance: Facilitation and Learned Helplessness", *Journal of Personality and Social Psychology, 24*, 132-42.

Rotter, J.B. (1966). "Generalised Expectancies for Internal Versus External Control of Reinforcement", *Psychological Monographs, 80* (Whole No. 609).

Rotter, J.B., Chance, J.E., and Phares, E.J. (1972). *Applications of Social Learning Theory of Personality*, New York: Holt, Rinehart & Winston.

Rotter, J.B., Seeman, M., and Liverant, S. (1962). "Internal Versus External Control of Reinforcement: A Major Variable in Behaviour

Theory", in N.F. Washburne (Ed.), *Decisions, Values and Groups (Vol. 2)*, Oxford: Perganon Press.

Sahoo, F.M. (1985a). *Cognitive Measure of Helplessness*. An unpublished report, Psychology Department, Utkal University, Bhubaneswar, India.

Sahoo, F.M. (1985b). *Children's Helplessness Questionnaire* (Oriya version). An unpublished report, Psychology Department, Utkal University, Bhubaneswar, India.

Sahoo, F.M. (1987). *Control, Agency and Means-ends Questionnaire* (Oriya-version). An unpublished report, Psychology Department, Utkal University, Bhubaneswar, India.

Sahoo, F.M. (1990). *Health Behaviour Questionnaire*. Unpublished manuscript, Psychology Department, Utkal University, Bhubaneswar, India.

Sahoo, F.M. (1991). "Learned Helplessness in Organizations", *Management and Labour Studies, 16(1)*, 1-10.

Sahoo, F.M. (1992). *The Student Behaviour Checklist (Oriya version)*. An unpublished report, Psychology Department, Utkal University, Bhubaneswar, India.

Sahoo, F.M. (1999). "Psychological Well-being of the Aged of Orissan Families", in J.R. Baral and A. Chowdhury (Eds.), *Family in Transition: Power and Development*, New Delhi: Northern Book Centre.

Sahoo, F.M. (2000). "Combating Alienation and Helplessness in Administrative Organization", *Journal of Community Guidance and Research, 17(1)*, 76-95.

Sahoo, F.M., and Acharya, B. (1996). *Learned Helplessness in Children: A Study of Perceived Control, Attributional Style, and Achievement*. An unpublished report, Psychology Department, Utkal University, Bhubaneswar, India.

Sahoo, F.M., Batra, G. (1997). "Self-efficacy and Attributional Styles in Mastery-oriented and Learned Helpless Students", *Indian Educational Review, 32(2)*, 91-103.

Sahoo, F.M., and Das, J. (1989). *The Role of Child Rearing Practices in the Development of Children's Helplessness*. Unpublished report, Psychology Department, Utkal University, Bhubaneswar, India.

Sahoo, F.M., and Kar, A. (1992). "Socialization Parameters of Children's Helplessness". Unpublished report, Psychology Department, Utkal University, Bhubaneswar, India.

Sahoo, F.M., and Kar, A. (1996). "Socialization Parameters of Learned Helplessness: Critical Dimensions of Maternal Interaction as Perceived by Children", *Indian Psychologist, 8*, 30-38.

Sahoo, F.M., and Mohapatra, C. (1992). *Learned Helplessness, Explanatory Styles, and Coping Patterns in Adolescents*. An unpublished report, Department of Psychology, Utkal University, Bhubaneswar, India.

Sahoo, F.M., and Nanda, B. (2000). "Role of Maternal Antecedents in the Development of Children's Competence". Unpublished report, Psychology Department, Utkal University, Bhubaneswar, India.

Sahoo, F.M., Nanda, S., and Sia, N. (1995). "Learned Helplessness and Work Involvement in Administrative and Financial Organizations", *Sankalpa, 3(2)*, 51-64.

Sahoo, F.M., and Nanda, U. (1988). "Socialization Parameters of Learned Helplessness", *Psychological Studies, 35*, 52-61.

Sahoo, F.M. and Paikray, P. (1994). *Maternal Antecedents of Children's Helplessness*. Unpublished report, Utkal University, Bhubaneswar, India.

Sahoo, F.M. and Panda, J. (1994). "Hospitalization and Helplessness", *Indian Psychologist, 7*, 10-20.

Sahoo, F.M., and Rath, S. (1989). "Learned Helplessness in School Students", *The Creative Psychologist, 1(2)*, 81-90.

Sahoo, F.M., and Ray, S.N. (1995). "Learned Helplessness and Work Involvement in Military Personnel". Unpublished report, Utkal University, Bhubaneswar, India.

Sahoo, F.M., and Sahoo, M. (1991). "Psychosocial Factors of Human Helplessness". An unpublished report, Psychology Department, Utkal University, Bhubaneswar, India.

Sahoo, F.M., and Sia, N. (1988). "The Socio-cultural Antecedents of Helplessness Among Rural Adolescents", *Indian Journal of Community Guidance Service, 5(1)*, 33-47.

Sahoo, F.M., and Sia, N. (1990). *Role of Socio-cultural Antecedents in the Development of Helplessness*. Unpublished report, Psychology Department, Utkal University, Bhubaneswar, India.

Sahoo, F.M., and Tripathy, B. (1993). *Motivational Antecedents of Academic Success: A Study of Children Learned Helplessness, Explanatory Style and Achievement*. Unpublished report, Psychology Department, Utkal University, Bhubaneswar, India.

Sahoo, F.M., and Tripathy, S. (1990). "Learned Helplessness in Industrial Employees: A Study of Non-contingency, Satisfaction and Motivational Deficits", *Psychological Studies, 35(2)*, 79-87.

Sarason, S.B., Davidson, K.S., Lighthall, F.F., Waite, R.R. and Ruebush, B.K. (1960). *Anxiety in Elementary School Children: A Report of Research*, New York: Wiley.

Schneewind, K.A. (1993). *Impact of Family Processes on Self-efficacy.* A paper presented at the Johann Jacops Foundation Conference on Self-efficacy in Adaptation of Youth to Changing Societies, Marbach, Germany.

Schneider, K. (1973). *Motivation,* Gottingen: Hogrofe.

Schulz, R. (1976). "Effect of Control and Predictability on the Physical and Psychological Well-being of the Institutionalised Aged", *Journal of Personality and Social Psychology, 33*, 563-73.

Schulz, R. (1978). *The Psychology of Death, Dying, and Bereavement,* Reading Mass: Addison-Wesley.

Schulz, R. (1980). "Aging and Control", in J. Ganber and M.E.P. Seligman (Eds.), *Human Helplessness: Theory and Applications,* New York: Academic Press.

Schunk, D.H. (1981). "Modelling and Attributional Feedback Effect on Children's Achievement: A Self-efficacy Analysis", *Journal of Educational Psychology, 74*, 93-105.

Schunk, D.H. (1982). "Effects of Effort Attributional Feedback on Children's Perceived Self-efficacy and Achievement", *Journal of Educational Psychology, 74*, 548-56.

Schunk, D.H. (1987). "Peer Models and Children's Behavioural Change", *Review of Educational Research, 57*, 149-74.

Schunk, D.H. (1989). "Self-efficacy and Achievement Behaviours", *Educational Psychology Review, 84*, 191-15.

Schunk, D.H. (1991). "Self-efficacy and Academic Motivation", *Educational Psychologist, 26*, 207-31.

Schunk, D.H., and Cox, P.D. (1986). "Strategy Training and Attributional Feedback with Learning Disabled Students", *Journal of Educational Psychology, 78*, 201-09.

Schunk, D.H., and Gunn, T.P. (1986). "Self-efficacy and Skill Development: Influence of Task Strategies and Attributions", *Journal of Educational Research, 79*, 238-44.

Schunk, D.H., and Rice, J.M. (1986). "Extended Attributional Feedback: Sequence Effects during Remedial Reading Instruction", *Journal of Early Adolescence, 6*, 55-66.

Schwartz, D.A. (1964). "The Paranoid-Depressive Existential Continuum", *Psychiartric Quarterly, 38*, 690-706.

Seligman, M.E.P. (1968). "Chronic Fear Produced by Unpredictable Electric Shock", *Journal of Comparative and Physiological Psychology, 66*, 402-11.

Seligman, M.E.P. (1974). "Depression and Learned Helplessness", in R.J. Friedman and M.M. Katz (Eds.), *The Psychology of Depression: Contemporary Theory and Research*, Washington: V.H. Winston.

Seligman, M.E.P. (1975). *Helplessness: On Depression Development and Death*, San Francisco: N.H. Freeman.

Seligman, M.E.P., Abramson, L.Y., Semmel, A., and van Baeyer, C. (1979). "Depressive Attributional Style", *Journal of Abnormal Psychology, 88*, 242-47.

Seligman, M.E.P., and Maier, S.F. (1967). "Failure to Escape Traumatic Shock", *Journal of Experimental Psychology, 74*, 1-9.

Seligman, M.E.P., Peterson, C., Kaslow, N.J., Tanenbaum, R.L., Alloy, L.B., and Abramson, L.Y. (1984). "Attributional Style and Depressive Symptoms among Children", *Journal of Abnormal Psychology, 93*, 253-38.

Serbin, L.A., O'Leary, K.D., Kent, R.N., and Tonick, I.O. (1973). "A Comparison of Teacher Response to the Pre-academic and Problem Behaviour of Boys and Girls", *Child Development, 44*, 796-804.

Shaw, B.F. (1977). "Comparison of Cognitive Therapy and Behaviour Therapy in the Treatment of Depression", *Journal of Consulting and Clinical Psychology, 45*, 543-51.

Sia, N., and Sahoo, F.M. (1991). "Combating Children's Learned Helplessness", *Indian Journal of Social Work, 52(3)*, 325-36.

Sia, N., Sahoo, F.M., and Sia, S.K. (1998). "Parental Expectancy and Children's Learned Helplessness", *Social Science International, 14(1&2)*, 19-28.

Silver, R.L., and Wortman, C.B. (1980). "Coping with Undesirable Life Events", in J. Garber, and M.E.P. Seligman (Eds.), *Human Helplessness: Theory and Application*, (pp. 279-340), London: Academic Press.

Silver, R.L., Wortman, C.B., and Klos, D.S. (1982). "Cognitions, Affect, and Behaviour following Uncontrollable Outcomes: A Response to Current Human Helplessness Research", *Journal of Personality, 30*, 480-514.

Singhal, S., and Kanungo, R. (1994a). "Attributional Model of Learned Helplessness in University Context"—Some Pointers", *Psychological Studies, 39*, 50-65.

Singhal, S., and Kanungo, R.N. (1994b). "Learned Helplessness Among Canadian and Indian Studies", *Psychologie, 37*, 95-103.

Singhal, S., and Kanungo, R.N. (1996). "Learned Helplessness Among University Student: A Bi-national Test of the Attributional Model", *Psychologia, 39*, 42-49.

Sinha, J.B.P. (1970). *Development through Behaviour Modification*, Bombay: Allied Publishers.

Skinner, EA. (1986). "The Origins of Young Children's Perceived Control, Mother Contingent and Sensitive Behaviour", *International Journal of Behavioural Development, 9*, 359-82.

Skinner, EA., and Chapman, M. (1984). "Control Beliefs in an Action Perspective", *Human Development, 77*, 129-33.

Skinner, EA., Chapman, M., and Baltes, P.B. (1988). "Control, Means—ends, and Agency Beliefs: A New Conceptualization and Its Measurement during Childhood", *Journal of Personality and Social Psychology, 54*, 119-33.

Skinner, EA., Wellborn, J.G., and Connell, J.P. (1990). "What it Takes to do Well in School and Whether I have Got It: A Process Model of Perceived Control and Children's Engagement and Achievement in School", *Journal of Educational Psychology, 82*, 22-32.

Smith, B.L., Wils, G., and Naylor, D. (1981). "The Effects of Parental Stress on Rate of Offsprings Learning Ability", *The Journal of Psychology, 107*, 45-51.

Smits, S.J. (1974). "Variables Related to Success in a Medical Rehabilitation Setting", *Archives of Physical Medicine and Rehabilitation, 55*, 449-54.

Snyder, M.L., Smoller, B., Srenta, A., and Frankl, A. (1981). "A Comparison of Egotism, Negativity, and Learned Helplessness as Explanations of Poor Performance after Unsolvable Problems", *Journal of Personality and Social Psychology, 10*, 24-30.

Stanley, M.A., and Maddux, J.E. (1986a). "Cognitive Processes in Health Enhancement: Investigation of a Combined Protection Motivation and Self-efficacy Model", *Basic and Applied Social Psychology, 7*, 101-13.

Stanley, M.A., and Maddux, J.E. (1986b). "Self-efficacy Expectancy and Depressed Mood: An Investigation of Causal Relationships", *Journal of Social Behaviour and Personality, 4*, 575-86.

Stevenson, H.W., Hale, G.A., Klein, R.E., and Miller, L.K. (1968). "Interrelations and Correlates in Children's Learning and Problem Solving", *Monographs of the Society of Research in Child Development, 33* (7, Serial No. 123).

Storms, M.D., and Nisbett, R.E. (1970). Insomnia and the Attribution Process", *Journal of Personality and Social Psychology, 11*, 319-28.

Strickland, B.R. (1978). "Internal-external Expectancies and Health Related Behaviours", *Journal of Consulting and Clinical Psychology, 46*, 1192-1211.

Strickland, B.R. (1979). "Internal-external Expectancies and Cardiovascular Functioning", in L.G. Penlmutter and R.A. Monty (Eds.), *Choice and Perceived Control*, Hillsdale, N.J.: Lawrence Erlbaum Assoc.

Sullivan, H.S. (1953). *The Interpersonal Theory of Psychiatry*, New York: Norton.

Taylor, F.C., and Marshall, W.L. (1977). "Experimental Analysis of Cognitive-behavioural Therapy for Depression", *Cognitive Therapy and Research, 1*, 59-72.

Taylor, S.E. (1979). "Hospital Patient Behaviour: Reactance, Helplessness, or Control?" *Journal of Social Issue, 35*, 156-84.

Taylor, S.E., and Crocker, J. (1980). "Schematic Bases of Social Information Processing", in E.T. Higgirs, C.P. Herman, and M.P. Zonna (Eds.), *Social Cognition: The Ontario Symposium*, Hillsdale, N.J.: Erlbaum.

Tennen, H., Drum, P.E., Gillen, R., and Stanton, A. (1982a). "Learned Helplessness and Detection of Contingency: A Direct Test", *Journal of Personality, 50*, 426-42.

Tennen, H., and Eller, S.J. (1977). "Attributional Components of Learned Helplessness and Facilitation", *Journal of Personality and Social Psychology, 35*, 265-71.

Tennen, H., Gillen, R., and Dnum, R.E. (1982b). "The Debilitating Effect of Exposure to Non-contingent Escape: A Test of the Learned Helplessness Model", *Journal of Personality, 50*, 409-25.

Tetrick, L.E., and LaRocco, J.M. (1987). "Understanding, Prediction, and Control as Moderators of the Relationships between Perceived Stress, Satisfaction and Psychological Well-being", *Journal of Applied Psychology, 72*, 538-43.

Tower, R.B., and Singer, J.L. (1981). "The Measurement of Emergency: How Can It be Clinically Useful?" in P.C. Kendall and S.D. Hollon (Eds.), *Assessment Strategies for Cognitive-Behavioural Interventions*, New York: Academic Press.

Triandis, H.C. (1993). "Collectivism and Individualism as Cultural Syndromes", *Cross-Cultural Research, 27*, 155-80.

Valins, S. and Nisbett, R.E. (1972). "Attribution Processes in the Development and Treatment of Emotional Disorder", in E.E. Jones, D.E. Kanouse, H.H. Kelley, R.E. Nisbett, S. Valins, and B. Weiner (Eds.), *Attribution: Perceiving the Causes of Behaviour*, Morristown, New Jersey: General Learning Press.

Veroff, J. (1969). "Social Comparison and Development of the Achievement Motivation", in C.P. Smith (Ed.), *Achievement-related Motives in Children*, New York: Russell Sage.

Verwoerdt, A., and Elmore, J.L. (1967). "Psychological Reaction in Fatal Illness: The Prospect of Impending Death", *Journal of the American Geratrics Society, 15*, 9-19.

Wallston, A.K. and Wallston, B.S. (1981). "Health Locus of Control Scales", in H.M. Lefcount (Ed.), *Research with the Locus of Control Construct* (Vol. 1), New York: Academic Press.

Watson, J.S. (1966). "The Development and Generalization of 'Contingency Awareness' in Early Infancy: Some Hypotheses", *Memill-Palmer Quarterly, 12*, 123-35.

Watson, J.S. (1971). "Cognitive Perceptual Development in Infancy: Setting for the Seventies", *Memill-Palmer Quarterly, 17*, 139-52.

Watson, J.S. (1977). "Depression and the Perception of Control in Early Childhood", in J.G. Schulterbrandt, A. Raskin (Eds.) *Depression in Childhood: Diagnosis, Treatment and Conceptual Models* (pp. 129-39), New York: Raven Press.

Watson, J.S., and Ramey, C.T. (1972). "Reactions to Response-contingent Stimulation in Early Infancy", *Memill-Palmer Quarterly, 18*, 219-27.

Weaver, C.N. (1977). "Relationships among Pay, Race, Sex, Occupational Prestige, Supervision, Work Autonomy, and Job Satisfaction in a National Sample", *Personnel Psychology, 30*, 437-45.

Weigel, L., Wertlieb, D., and Feldstein, M. (1989). "Perception of Control, Competence and Contingency as Influences on the Stress-behaviour Symptom Relation in School-age Children", *Journal of Personality and Social Psychology, 56*, 456-64.

Weiner, B. (1972). *Theories of Motivation: From Mechanism to Cognition*, Chicago: Rand McNally.

Weiner, B. (1974). *Achievement Motivation and Attribution Theory*, Morristown, N.J.: General Learning Press.

Weiner, B. (1979). "A Theory of Motivation for Same Classroom Experiences", *Journal of Educational Psychology, 71*, 3-25.

Weiner, B. (1985a). "Spontaneous". Causal Search. *Psychological Bulletin, 97*, 74-84.

Weiner, B. (1985b). "An Attributional Theory of Achievement Motivation and Emotion", *Psychological Review, 92*, 548-73.

Weiner, B., Frieze, I., Kukla, A., Reed, L., Rest, S., and Rosenbaum, R.M. (1971). *Perceiving the Causes of Success and Failure*, Morristown, N.J.: General Learning Process.

Weiner, B., and Litman-Adizen, T. (1980). "An Attributional Expectancy—Value Analysis of Learned Helplessness and Depression", in J. Garber and M.E.P. Seligman (Eds.), *Human Helplessness: Theory and Applications*, New York: Academic Press.

Weiner, B., Nierenberg, R., and Goldstein, M. (1976). "Social Learning (Locus of Control) Versus Attributional (Causal Stability) Interpretations of Expectancy of Success", *Journal of Personality, 44*, 52-68.

Weiss, J.M. (1970). "Somatic Effects of Predictable and Unpredictable Shock", *Psychomatic Medicine, 32*, 397-408.

Weiss, J.M. (1971). "Effects of Coping Behavior in Different Warning Signal Conditions on Stress Pathology in Rats", *Journal of Comparative and Physiological Psychology, 77*, 1-30.

Weiss, J.M. (1972). "Psychological Factors in Stress and Disease", *Scientific American, 226*, 104-13.

Weiss, J.M. and Glazer, H.L. (1975). "Effects of Acute Exposure to Stressors on Subsequent Avoidance-escape Behavior", *Psychosomatic Medicine, 37*, 499-521.

Weiss, J.W., Glazer, H.L., and Poboresky, L.A. (1976). "Coping Behaviour and Neurochemical Changes in Rats: An Alternative Explanation for the Original 'Learned Helplessness' Experiments", in G. Serban and A. King (Eds.), *Annual Models in Human Psychology*, New York: Plenum.

Weiss, J.M., Stone, E.A., and Harrell, N. (1970). "Coping Behaviour and Brain Norepinephrine Level in Rats", *Journal of Comparative and Psychological Psychology, 72*, 153-60.

Wellborn, J.G., Connell, J.P., and Skinner, E.A. (1989). *The Student Perception of Control Questionnaire*, Rochester, New York: University of Rochester.

White, R.W. (1959). "Motivation Reconsidered: The Concept of Competence", *Psychological Review, 66*, 297-333.

Whiting, B.B., Child, I.L., Lambert, W.W., and Whiting, J.W.W. (1963). *Six Cultures: Studies of Child Rearing*, New York: Willey.

Whiting, B.B., and Whitting, J.W.M. (1975). *Children of Six Cultures: A Psycho-cultural Analysis*, Cambridge, Mass: Harvard University Press.

Whiting, J.W.M. (1981). "Environmental Constraints on Infant Care Practices", in R.H. Munroe, R.L. Munroe and B.B. Whiting (Ed.), *Handbook of Cross-cultural Human Development*, New York: Ganland STPM Press.

Whiting, J.W.M., and Child, I.L. (1953). *Child Training and Personality*, New Haven: Yale University Press.

Williams, J.W.M., and Spitzer, R.L. (1983). "The Issue of Sex Bias in DSM-111", *American Psychologist, 38*, 793-98.

Wilson, J. (1972). *Patterns of Mathematics Achievements in Grades: Z Population*. Paper presented for National Institute of Education, U.S.A.

Wilson, T.D., and Linville, P.W. (1982). "Improving the Academic Performance of College Freshman: Attribution Theory Revisited", *Journal of Personality and Social Psychology, 42*, 367-76.

Wilson, T.D. and Linville, P.W. (!985). "Improving the Performance of College Freshmen with Attributional Techniques", *Journal of Personality and Social Psychology, 49*, 282-93.

Winett, R.A., King, A.C., Altman, D.G. (1983). *Health Psychology and Public Health*, New York: Pergaman Press.

Winterbottom, M.R. (1958). "The Relation of Need for Achievement to Learning Experience in Independence and Mastery", in J.W. Atkinson (Ed.), *Motives of Fantasy, Action and Society* (pp. 454-78), Princeton, New Jersey: Van Nostrand.

Witkin, H.A., and Berry, J.W. (1975). "Psychological Differentiation in Cross Cultural Perspective", *Journal of Cross-Cultural Psychology, 6*, 4-87.

Woolfolk, A.E., and Hoy, W.K. (1990). "Perspective Teachers' Sense of Efficacy and Belief about Control", *Journal of Educational Psychology, 82*, 81-91.

Wortman, C.B. (1976). "Causal Attributions and Personal Control", in J. Harvey, W. Ickes, and R.T. Kidds (Eds.), *New Directions in Attribution Research*, Hillsdale, N.J.: Lawrence Erlbaum Associates.

Wortman, C.B. and Dintzer, L. (1978). "Is An Attributional Analysis of the Learned Helplessness Phenomenon Viable?: A Critique of the Abramson-Seligman-Teasdale Reformulation", *Journal of Abnormal Psychology, 87*, 75-90.

Wortman, C.B., Panciera, L., Shusterman, L., and Hibscher, J. (1976). "Attributions of Causality and Reactions to Uncontrollable Outcomes", *Journal of Experimental Social Psychology, 12*, 301-16.

Wright, L. (1988). "The Type A Behaviour Pattern and Coronary Artery Disease: Quest for the Active Ingredients and the Elusive Mechanism", *American Psychologist, 43*, 1-3.

Yarrow, L.J. (1961). "Maternal Deprivation: Toward an Empirical and Conceptual Revolution", *Psychological Bulletin, 58*, 469-70.

Zimmerman, B.J., and Ringle, J. (1981). "Effects of Persistence and Statements of Confidence on Children's Self-efficacy and Problem Solving", *Journal of Educational Psychology, 73*, 485.

Zuckerman, M. and Lubin, B. (1965). *Manual for the Multiple Affect Adjective Check List*, San Diego, California: Educational and Industrial Testing Service.

INDEX